M000044981

Thank
for your support
From Mr Fresh ♡.

#MomBoss

Inspirational stories of Mommy Managers helping their children build businesses, manage money and develop confidence through entrepreneurship.

collaboration presented by
Arriel Biggs

chapters by
Aunkule Benford-Campbell | Arriel Biggs
Landra Cannon | Shay Danrich | Sauywanna Davis
Latrice Floyd | Cecilia Rigsby | Tamishio Hawkins
Nia Lewis | Tanika Prowell | Tamara M. Robinson

Dedicated to all of the moms who juggle home, personal and professional lives each day and still make time to help their children and community by introducing young entrepreneurs into our society. You are truly appreciated!

- Mom Boss-es

Introduction

When we hear the word Boss, we think of a person who is in control or in a position of authority. This person supervises and directs those that have authority over others to achieve excellence and growth. Further considering this word, one may take a closer look by closing their eyes and visualizing a "boss" to be a male, maybe with a suit sitting in a big office. Well this book is evidence that picture is changing because women are now expanding the vision of a Boss! Women are starting their own businesses and employing more people, which help them support more households. In addition, many women do this as moms while raising children, running their households and maintaining their marriages. This is why boss has been given a new definition - (B.O.S.S. - Bold Omnipresent Sassy and Successful). This new definition came to light during my first book collaboration #BossMoms. This best-selling book was a collaboration of 10 women who shared their story of how they pursued their dreams to start a business while raising their families. The #BossMoms movement was a unique platform for women to be their own B.O.S.S. (Bold Omnipresent Sassy and Successful).

Having such great success the first time around with book collaborations; Arriel Biggs – the real B.O.S.S. is at it again! Arriel has now spearheaded her own book collaboration, #MomBoss with 10 more unique women (mommy managers) who share their stories of how they helped their children build businesses, manage money and develop confidence through entrepreneurship. Arriel's own personal story of being a "mommy manager" led her to take on this project. Arriel agrees that it is time for moms with children entrepreneurs to live their dreams out loud in her book collaboration #MomBoss. Arriel states, "It's Winning Season. It's time for the #MomBoss everywhere to be BOLD, OMNI-PRESENT, SASSY, and SUCCESSFUL."

-Deletra Hudson, MBA
"The Financial Educator"

TABLE OF CONTENTS

Foreward

And this is how the story begins...

You
will meet warriors and champions that ride for not
only the dreams of their children but for their own
personal success and wellness.

These
moms are done being victims of circumstance, done
working hard just to survive. These moms are
thriving and building their family units and legacy.

As
the mom of one of the most successful teenagers in
the country, I am all too familiar with the struggles
related to parenting, business, balance and more.

Listen,
my struggle list at one time was long too. The thing
is, I grew through them, they changed my life,
enhanced my vision and strengthened my parenting
and business muscles. So as you work through your
own struggles I will ask you to do a few things,
assuming you are interested in becoming a
#MOMBOSS yourself while maintaining your
current status.

As
you read through the following stories of parenting, perseverance, and power; please consider yourself. What can you do better? What have you mastered? In what ways can you work toward maintaining a healthy, nurturing environment for your children and yourself?

I'm not asking you to compare your life to theirs, I am asking that you allow your mind, heart, and spirit to be open.

I
challenge you to look at your child(ren) as momentum in this world. They are the development of your process, which means your process needs to be consistent and honest.

Learn
yourself before forcing them to become themselves.

Approach
all situations with love, light, and understanding.

Ask
yourself often. "what could I have done if I had gotten the support I needed?"

I
want you also focus on being a "good enough" mom, NOT a perfect one. That alone will kill your

spirit on a daily basis, which will spill over to your child. You are enough. Believe that and own it. This book is an opportunity to take a behind the scenes look at moms that are doing what you are doing or hoping to do.

Take
what you need and stick a pin in what you may not be ready for. Embrace this as your journey, your process to enough.

Now
you get to choose how this story ends.

My
name is Tamara Zantell and I am a #MOMBOSS

Tamara Zantell is a mother to 5 superstar changemakers. As a licensed mortuary scientist with a degree in business management, she worked for over 10 years as a management consultant and small business strategist in both the medical and restaurant fields in addition to 15 years as the Chief Operating Officer for the largest medical specialty practices in Western New York. She helped clients build strong community relationships, deliver excellent service while building well managed diverse environments via culture, goals, and structure.

As an official corporate dropout, Tamara has helped her teenage daughter, Zandra A. Cunningham, turn her kitchen table hobby and turn it into a million dollar brand. Tamara has advanced knowledge in launching an international brand, generating revenue, partnership development, and preparing young moguls for success.

As the founder of Raising A Mogul, LLC and the CEO of RAM Brand Management, a strategic brand management & consulting firm, Tamara is committed to supporting parents with the confidence, knowledge, and tools they need to Raise Young Moguls.

tamaarzantell.com
/ @tamaarzantell

raisingamogul.com
/ @raisingamogul

Join our free community at
www.raisingamogul.org

Arriel Biggs
Entrepreneur, Author and Speaker

Arriel is the founder and executive director of
Young Biz Kidz, a nonprofit organization whose
mission is to empower young people by engaging
and encouraging financial literacy and
entrepreneurship in youth. She believes that teaching
financial education through entrepreneurship is a
great way to introduce smart money habits early. As
the momager of *Mikey...The Kid who Knows the Biz*
(her son and child business owner), Arriel works to
help other families see that business ownership and
financial freedom is an option for everyone.

In addition to providing income, Arriel wants all to
know that entrepreneurship teaches effective
communication, personal responsibilities, and

problem solving skills. It also builds self-esteem and strong relationships making it a great resource economically, academically and socially.

Initially focusing on educating youth, Arriel soon realized that parents could also use guidance in helping their children become business owners. She now offers services to educate, empower and equip parents with the self-confidence to support their Biz Kid.

Always on the go, Arriel is a mentor, child advocate, parent advisor, public speaker, and currently serves as the Midwest Chapter President for Raising A Mogul Society.

She has received many accolades for being a phenomenal woman entrepreneur and has been requested to share her knowledge with local, national and international audiences. One of her most cherished awards is for her chapter titled *#MomBoss* as a co-author of the bestselling book #BossMom.

Arriel has taken her role as Mom Boss to another level and began empowering moms and families to become the boss in their lives.

I Am Arriel Biggs - Mom Boss

Raising Money Savvy Kidz
by Arriel Biggs

"Failure is an important part of your growth and developing resilience. Don't be afraid to fail." –
Michelle Obama

There is no secret that most Americans lack financial education. If you are anything like me, you grew up in a household where we didn't talk about money. I remember getting my first job, I was extremely excited. I laid out my pants, placed my work hat on top of my polo style work shirt all in preparation for my first day. My work schedule was the center of attraction in my bedroom. I posted it proudly on my bedroom wall every week, being careful to plan around school and my sports schedule. I worked 4-hour shifts on weekdays and 8-hour shifts on the weekends in order to have money to buy all the things I needed from the mall. I would walk through the shopping center before work and make mental notes of all the things I had to have and checked them off my list such as Polo, Levi's, and Nike Air Max.

I was 16 years old with no real responsibilities but buying nice clothes to wear to the skating rink on Friday and Saturday nights. Looking back, I now understand how financial principals and money management could have made my life very different. I understand now that most of our parents didn't know how to teach us to be successful financially.

The Talk

In my household growing up, we didn't talk about money, but we sure knew when it was payday! Our whole family went out to eat (*sometimes to Chuck E. Cheese*), shopping, the movies, bumper cars, etc. What we didn't know was that there were many bills that were paid before we could do fun things, *or* if those bills were even paid before we celebrated. I know my parents loved us and wanted us to have the best life possible. I'm pretty sure you want the same for your kids.

If we are going to give our children a better life than we had, we have to make sure we as parents have an understanding of financial principals and money management. It's up to us to give them a solid understanding of basic financial education. There is no big secret to creating financial success for you and your children. The formula is pretty simple.

First, educate your children on how money works. Second, equip them with entrepreneurship as a tool for success. Last, empower by allowing them to make age-appropriate decisions in life and business.

Educating Your Child About Money

Yes, it's time for us as parents to teach our children about money and money management. I remember having a conversation with a friend. I stated, "it's a shame schools aren't teaching our children about money, that's so sad." I remember feeling as if it was the school's fault that when I was young I didn't know what I was supposed to know about money. Since my parents never really spoke to me about finances, I assumed that the school would be the institution to prepare me and others.

After taking a moment, I remember asking myself "why am I putting *my* responsibility on the school for *my* child's lack of financial knowledge?" What I hadn't initially realized was that by blaming the school for my child's lack of financial awareness, I was giving my power over to the system. I made up my mind that I was going to take responsibility for my child and not leave it up to any other institution. Money management had to start at home, so I focused on ways to introduce money to my child early. I started allowing my son to make a list of items he needed, select those items at the store and pay for them at the checkout counter. I started this process when my son was 6 years old. He soon became comfortable with shopping for himself and now even looks for coupons to save money.

Teaching children about money early should not be an afterthought, it is just as important as ABC's and 123's. I let my children know that understanding reading, writing, and math is a big part of being financially successful. I let them know that it's not about the money that they make, it's about how much of it they keep and how well they manage what they earn.

The Present and the Future

Our children should understand that no matter who you are or where you grew up, most Americans have the same two financial goals.

- First, I have noticed that just about everyone wants to protect and maintain their family lifestyle with the money they are making. For example, within your income you want to be able to buy a house, car, pay bills and still have money to take family trips and go out to eat.

- Secondly, most people want to take care of their *future* lifestyle with investments.

Most parents I talk with are meeting the first goal, but not the second. When I started working, I had no idea what a 401k, IRA or any financial terms meant. At the time, the job where I worked matched up to 4% of employee's retirement investments. I worked for more than ten years before I started investing in my 401k. I realized I was giving up free money. Moms and Dads this is really important for your children to understand. The return on investment (ROI) must be managed; a portion of it should go into an account to help it grow and be put away for the future. I know if you are anything like me you don't want your children to have to work all their adult years and retire just to go back to work to maintain their lifestyle at that time. That is why, teaching good money habits early are key to preparing our children for financial success.

Understanding Challenges We All Face

I thought cutting off my cable, not going out to eat and curbing my shopping was the answer to good money management, but I noticed I felt as if I was missing out on something. I was saving, but I was not enjoying my life. It wasn't until I became aware of some of the obstacles we all face that make it difficult to hit our financial goals and allow us to live life more abundantly.

What I discovered was that these obstacles, like so many others, impress themselves on everyone. These barriers to me accumulating money were impacting my ability to save, mainly because I was not accounting for their presence in my budget. I continued to have unexpected expenditures and thought it was all due to frivolous spending. Instead, I learned that I was not forecasting my expenses fully nor tracking where money was being required.

For Example:

1. Inflation 2. Taxes 3. Income Taxes 4. Debt 5. Holiday Spending (January - New Year, February - Valentine Day, March - St. Patrick's Day, April - Easter, May - Mother's Day, June - Father's Day, July - Independence Day, August - Back to School, September - Labor Day, October - Halloween, November - Thanksgiving and the Amazing Black Friday and December -Christmas)

I had to shift my mindset if I wanted to start living a financially successful life. I knew *how* to make money. I just didn't know how to *manage* the money I made.

Spending with a Purpose

Once I became educated, it empowered me to make changes and equipped me with financial understanding. I talked with my husband and we agreed to start teaching our children early. We decided to start buying gifts for the children that would produce more money for them in the future. For example, Mikey got vending machines two Christmases in a row. We explained to him why and he told us he understood. Our focus is not on the money he makes. It's that he understands how to make money work for him. We believe if you start teaching smart money habits early the children will be able to structure their financial live much better.

I laugh when I reflect back on how I would spend money on things that I was convinced my children had to have. I bought them all the toys and clothes I felt they deserved. I was playing into a global system that would ultimately lead to poverty if we kept it up. What my children truthfully deserved were parents that would spend time with them and were financially responsible.

In 2010 my husband and I decided we wanted to live more abundantly for ourselves and our children. Both he and I had traditional jobs and we both worked a lot. I would work overtime, my husband at one point was working two full-time jobs and we were still living paycheck to paycheck. We sat down planned our moves and stuck with it. For our plan to work we had to move in with my parents. It was a little embarrassing, but it put us in a position to stick to our goals. We set goals to buy a house and cars debt free. We were able to accomplish our goals in 18 months. We also took our son and my little cousin to Disney World during those 18 months.

We were able to start living our lives and enjoying our children without the worry of not being able to support them. By making the decision to step outside my comfort zone and walk by faith, it put us in a position to break generational cycles and to create a new set of traditions. By spending more time with my son, I was able to watch, help him to grow and experience the development of a young entrepreneur, author, and speaker at 8-years old. I'm waiting to see what my daughter will want to do. As a momager, I understand how powerful entrepreneurship can be when teaching life skills to youth and teaching parents how to engage with their children.

Use Entrepreneurship as a Parenting Tool to Engage with Your Child

I personally feel there are a ton of life skills that can be taught through entrepreneurship such as effective communication, personal responsibilities, problem-solving skills, self-esteem and teaching the importance of giving back. Two of the biggest things teaching through entrepreneurship has done for me was to allow me to engage with my children in what they were passionate about (even if they have a new idea every week). It's a good way for us as parents to show our children we believe in you, we are listening to you and we will support you, ultimately building a stronger family relationship and a more confident individual. The second way that entrepreneurship helped us was it gave our children a way to make their own money (strengthening pride of self).

I mentioned earlier that we were living paycheck to paycheck. We started teaching Cash-Asset-Cash to my son when he was 7 years old. I taught him that whenever he received cash he needed to buy or invest in something that would produce more cash. So, what he did was started a lemonade stand with one of his friends. They made $1200 running the stand in over 3 days. With the money, they made they donated 10% to a nonprofit and split the remainder down the middle. My son took his half of the money and invested in a vending machine business called Mikey's Munchies Vending. The company has grown to six full-service vending machines and a new sales department to sell Mikey's Munchies branded vending machines. In addition, Mikey wrote two children books to help his peers learn about entrepreneurship. The first book is called Mikey Learns about Business (written for 3rd-8th graders) and the other is Biz Is a Wiz (written for pre-K - 3rd graders). Mikey became a best-selling author at 10 years old. He was able to sell 1000 books in 5 months. He's proud of that accomplishment because most self-published authors will not sell over 1000 books. Mikey has won multiple awards and was named Honorary Junior Grand Marshal in the Ameren Thanksgiving Day Parade. He has traveled to many States sharing his story and inspiring other kids with his carefully chosen slogan, "Little People Can Do Big Things Too!"

Starting a business with Mikey and going through the entrepreneurial process helped me to better understand Mikey and it helps him to express himself with confidence while, learning different skill sets (video, social media marketing, finances, budgeting, etc.). Most importantly it gave me confidence as a Mom that Mikey has the right tools and skills to be successful in life.

The Unexpected

One of my biggest fears was something happening to me and not having an active role in preparing my children for life. In October 2017 that fear hit home, I was diagnosed with stage 3 breast cancer. My immediate thoughts were, my kids, my kids. I wanted to live for them, so I started my treatment plan. It included chemotherapy, a double mastectomy and reconstruction surgery - all treatment processes that were challenging and very intrusive.

As I stated before, the journey was challenging, and I was faced with several bumps in the road. It proved to be one of the most impactful and life changing ordeals I ever had to face with my children. What gave me comfort was that I was still able to watch my children grow and mature right before my eyes. My son never stopped running his business. At one of his events I found myself watching the camera man put a microphone on him, he seemed so confident, calm and cool in that moment. I continued watching him from afar with tears of joy in my eyes and an overwhelming sense of pride. He also stepped up his role around the house making small meals, doing laundry and reading with his younger sister at bedtime. Entrepreneurship helped me to prepare my son for adulthood.

3 Tips to Help You Get Your Biz Kid Started in Entrepreneurship

Tip 1. Have your child complete a business plan

The Business Plan

The business plan is a written document that describes an idea for a product or service and how it will make money. It includes your marketing plan as well as estimates for revenue, expenses, and how to make a profit. Help your Biz Kid understand that the business plan is like a GPS for their business. It helps them with the starting point and guides them to their destination which would be running a successful business.

Allowing your child to plan various aspects of their business on paper keeps them from making unnecessary mistakes later on. It also helps your Biz Kid think about the costs associated with starting a business and it shows you as parents that they are serious about their business idea.

Coming Up with An Idea and Business Name

First, you want to have a conversation about what the child's interest is. Next, help them figure out how they can break down their idea to start making money in 7 days. Figure out what products or services they will sell and who they will sell them to. This seems easy, but there are so many different directions to go in, which can seem overwhelming. That's why it is important to have a plan before you start so you won't get pulled in so many different directions.

Here's an example: Your child starts a baking business and decides to sell cookies, cupcakes, and brownies. How many different flavors of cookies, cupcakes, and brownies can you think of? Just that simple task can be overwhelming and a lot of work for a child. Here is how to simplify it. Have your child figure out the top three flavors in each category they would like to sell. Then put a plan together on how you will release other ideas later, one at a time

Tip 2. *Open a saving account*

Opening a saving account has many benefits. It keeps hard earned money safe and it earns interest. Overall, it's an important part of teaching kids about money and building community relations. Be sure to shop around to see what bank offers the best account to fit your child's needs.

Tip 3. *Have your elevator speech ready*

This speech is all about you, who you are, what you do, and what you want to do. Your elevator speech is a way to share your business with people who don't know you. And it's a great way to gain confidence while introducing yourself when growing your network. Practice, practice, practice is the best way to get comfortable with an elevator speech. You should practice with your child until it becomes natural for him/her, without sounding robotic and always have a business card ready.

3 Tips for Healthy Mommy Mangers

1. **Take time for yourself** - you are your child/ren's biggest supporter. Our kids need us to show up as our best selves. Physical, emotional mental and spiritual health is extremely important on this journey.

2. **We are moms first**- Protect your child/ren in this entrepreneurship space. If something doesn't sit right with you, trust your gut. Listen to your child and let your child/ren be the driving force behind the business. Be mindful of motives when people are trying to attach themselves to your child's business. Everything that glitters isn't gold.

3. **Find your tribe**- I'm a strong believer that we are better together. Finding a village of like-minded individuals will be beneficial in your journey. Include individuals that add value to your life and support you with love. Your tribe will become your biggest cheerleaders

Additional Tips for Managing Children

- Allow room in your child's schedule for entrepreneurial projects
- Develop Smart Goals with your child (Specific-Measurable-Achievable-Relevant-Timed)
- Let your child experiment with different areas of entrepreneurship
- Let your child be themselves
- For every corrected action, tell them two things they did well
- Celebrate all wins no matter how small

"And as we let our own light shine, we unconsciously give others permission to do the same. As we're liberated from our own fear, our presence automatically liberates others."- *Marianne Williamson*

For more information contact:
Email: arrielbiggs@gmail.com
Instagram/ Arriel Biggs
Facebook/ Arriel Biggs
YouTube/ Arriel Biggs
Website: ArrielBiggs.com

Tamishio Hawkins
Communications Specialist, Entrepreneur, Momager

Tamishio Hawkins is the mother of one and momager to Tamia Hawkins. Currently working in telecommunications, she spends most of her free time helping her 12 year old daughter run her business called Mia's Treats Delight where she sells her famous homemade cookies, brownies, and cupcakes.

Tamishio also serves on the board for Young Biz Kidz as the Parent Recruiter.

She attended the University of Missouri-Columbia where she studied Social Work & Psychology and often organizes events that focus on feeding the homeless and passing out clothing and toiletries.

Tamishio's passion and mission is to help others and she aspires to start her own nonprofit serving the homeless population.

I Am Tamishio Hawkins - Mom Boss

Vision with a Dash of Love and Support
by Tamishio Hawkins

"I've come to believe that each of us has a personal calling that's as unique as a fingerprint – and that the best way to succeed is to discover what you love and then find a way to offer it to others in the form of service, working hard, and also allowing the energy of the universe to lead you." — *Oprah Winfrey*

As parents, we naturally want what's best for our children, right? We want to give them what we never had, provide opportunities that we were never afforded, or just shower them with an abundance of love and affection that maybe we didn't receive growing up. Whatever the case may be, our children are our main priority and we'll do whatever it takes to help them reach their full potential.

Growing up, I was always taught that you graduate from high school, go to college, and get a job that pays well - the traditional route. I followed this formula and it served me well, but I was left with a lot of debt and a job that left me dissatisfied and unfulfilled. It was definitely not how I envisioned my adult life. With that being said, I always encouraged my daughter, Tamia, to own her own business when she became an adult and reassured her that she could do whatever she put her mind to.

As a child that's a natural leader, I informed Tamia that being an entrepreneur came with many perks like being your own boss, being able to make your own schedule, hiring your own employees, and the list goes on. To my surprise, when she was 8 years old, she came to me and said, "Mommy, I don't want to wait until I'm an adult to own my own business. I want to own my own business now." I will never forget those words or that moment. It absolutely blew my mind! Expressing her desires to me not only confirmed that she had been listening all those years prior, but it also brought me to the realization that I unknowingly placed limitations on her by simply telling her, "when you become an adult." Why wait until she becomes an adult to be a business owner? I did tell Tamia that she could do whatever she put her mind to, right?

Cooking up ideas

I proceeded to ask her what kind of business she wanted to open, and she told me a bakery. It made perfect sense because from the time Tamia was able to walk, she always loved being in the kitchen with me or my mother (affectionately known as "Nanny"). You could often find Tamia in the kitchen with her Nanny making chocolate chip cookies, brownies, and other sweet treats - some homemade, others made from the box. I told Tamia her idea was awesome, but she would have to learn how to bake from scratch because anyone can bake treats from the box. She simply said, "Ok!" She's always been up for a challenge, so I wasn't surprised with her enthusiastic response.

The day Tamia told me she wanted to open a bakery, we went to the store and picked up some basic things that she would need in order to bake. I must confess, I don't bake at all, so I found a chocolate cupcake recipe online and she made her first batch of homemade cupcakes. They turned out really good and she ended up selling them that evening! This particular recipe called for coffee, in which Tamia was not a fan of, so I contacted a friend of mine who's a baker and she shared some of her recipes for Tamia to try. She played around with each recipe until she got the results she was happy with. Tamia was 8 years old so initially I helped her with measurements and other things she would naturally need assistance with, but after a couple of months she was on her own and didn't need any assistance at all.

"Start where you are. Use what you have. Do what you can." -Arthur Ashe

Now, to be honest, when Tamia told me she wanted to start her own business, I was going through some financial difficulties, and quite frankly didn't have the extra money to go buy what she needed in order to start. I could have patted her on the back and told her that owning a bakery was a good idea and left it at that, but that would have negated everything I ever taught her. I decided to make a sacrifice in that moment and move on faith because our children are our biggest investment and you never know what can develop from lighting that little spark that's inside each & every one of our children. That sacrifice was probably the best decision I could have ever made.

The first 10 months were pretty rough for me because I was trying to keep up with the growing demand of Mia's products, not realizing that her products were well underpriced. While dozens of people were enjoying Mia's cookies, I was continuously falling behind on bills. Working a 9 to 5 and not knowing anything about running a business, let alone how much to charge for these delicious products, I reached out to a baker we met in Miami, Mrs. Charli, owner of the famous Cupcake Galleria. She was gracious enough to calculate how much Mia should have been charging for each of her products and needless to say, Mia was basically giving her baked goodies away for free. I was disappointed receiving this news, but I knew with this information we could make the proper adjustments and turn things around.

When we decided to increase the prices of Mia's products, I was a little worried that she would lose customers being that many had been paying the same amount for quite some time. To my surprise, this change actually came with a boost in sales and an increased number of new customers. With this, we were able to witness first hand that people are willing to pay good money as long as you have a good product and of course excellent customer service.

"It takes a village to raise a child." – African Proverb

I've always been adamant about surrounding my child with positive people who would stimulate growth as opposed to hindering it. For this very reason, I reached out to my friend Dani (the baker I previously mentioned who generously shared some of her recipes) asking if she could mentor my little aspiring baker. She happily agreed and came over once a month for two hours to shadow Tamia in the kitchen, giving her pertinent baking tips. Tamia started out with cupcakes and then moved on to brownies. After mastering brownies came the game changer... chocolate chip cookies.

As the official taste tester, everything she bakes is yummy, but I'm a cookie kind of girl so it was adios to any kind of waistline that I ever had when the cookies came on the scene! Tamia's cookies are by far the best cookies I've ever had and are her best seller (and that's without any bias). These delicious, heaven sent cookies really put her on the map. Tamia has been featured on Fox 2 News three times. She's been flown out to Miami, FL where she interviewed with Cupcake Galleria's owner, Mrs. Charli. While there, she baked cookies and brownies for children in Liberty City, FL and had a forum on entrepreneurship with them right in the middle of the neighborhood. It was refreshing to see her connecting with other children and being an inspiration while simply just doing what she loves and being a kid. She even spoke at the 2018 STL Women's March! Tamia has participated in countless vendor events and have met some of the most amazing people along the way.

In April of 2018, Tamia was the recipient of the Made Moguls Youth Entrepreneur Award. She even met and gave cookies to Luvvie Ajayi, Jussie Smollet, Mali Music, The Hamiltone's, and the talented singing married duo, Raii & Whitney.

These last few years have been very exciting. Tamia's schedule includes; meeting new people, traveling, invitations to different events and the list goes on. But let me be very clear. It hasn't been easy fulfilling the momager role, especially as a single parent. There have been countless long nights and stressful days. Many nights I went to sleep at 5:00am only to wake back up at 6:30am to get ready for an

31

event. Looking back, I'm not even sure how I made it at times. Being a full time momager of a young entrepreneur in addition to working a stressful full-time corporate job can take a toll on you. I quickly realized the importance of self-care and learned the art of saying "No." Trust me. It's imperative that you practice both.

Being a mom-ager

Tamia makes all of her batters herself, but I play the personal assistant role by putting batters in the oven for her while she works on new batters. I help decorate cupcakes, package orders, make store runs, and take her to meet customers. Imagine carrying out these duties, still working a 9 to 5, all while still dealing with the stressors of everyday life. There are times where I'm ready to quit, but I quickly remember that quitting is NOT an option. What message would I be sending my daughter? Quitting would discredit everything I ever told her, teaching Tamia that it's okay to throw in the towel when things get a little difficult. I often tell her that being an entrepreneur is going to be hard at times, but you have two options:

1. Work for someone else and have to deal with stress while being told when to come and go.

2. Be your own boss while dealing with some form of stress that you would have to deal with either way.

Don't get me wrong. If you work a 9 to 5 that's perfectly okay. I'm not job shaming. I still work a 9 to 5! I'm fully aware that entrepreneurship isn't for everyone and some thrive off the structure a 9 to 5 provides. As parents, we have to make sure we're listening to our children and paying close attention to those hobbies & interests that spark something inside of them. Help them cultivate those brilliant ideas because this is the time where they're the most creative. If we're honest with ourselves, a lot of adults are just as creative, but we let doubt, insecurities, that 9 to 5, or the opinions of others keep us from pursuing our passions and living out our dreams. Our children don't carry any of that dead weight so let's pour into them now so they can grow into bold & fearless adults.

"My mission in life is not merely to survive, but to thrive; and to do so with some passion, some compassion, some humor, and some style." -Maya Angelou

For more information contact:
Tamishio Hawkins
tdhawkins83@gmail.com

Tanika J. Prowell
Registered Nurse, Momager

Tanika J. Prowell is a Registered Nurse whose background includes Maternal-Child Health, Public Health, Medical-Surgical Nursing, and Correctional Nursing.

In 2005, Prowell graduated cum laude from the University of Missouri- Saint Louis with a Bachelor of Science in Nursing. She has been accepted into the graduate program at Tennessee State University and plans to pursue a Master's degree in Public Health. She currently provides nursing care and education to pregnant women, infants, and children through home visits.

Tanika is the devoted mother of two children, Joshua and Takiyah. She is also the "Momager" of Joshua's business, JZ's Sweets, which offers candy, cake pops, and other treats.

She has a passion for community outreach and has partnered with several faith-based, community, and social justice organizations.

Tanika is a member of Friendly Temple Missionary Baptist Church. She hopes to inspire others through her life story.

I am Tanika Prowell –Mom Boss

Make Time to Conquer the Impossible
by Tanika J. Prowell

*"With God all things are possible" –Matthew 19:26
KJV*

Imagine being fully responsible for the care of two young children, one full-time job, two part-time jobs, traveling back and forth between two states to check on loved ones, and oh, don't forget the unexpected trials and tribulations that life throws your way. Now think about all of the unwritten rules, responsibilities, and duties that motherhood brings, add your ten-year-old son telling you that he wants to start his own business. Seems like an impossible task, right? I didn't think that it would be possible to move forward with this idea due to what I perceived was a lack of time. Remember the game "Where's Waldo?" in which one would sometimes spend hours trying to find "Waldo" in a busy scene. That's how I feel about the concept of time. Where is it? How can I get more of it? If I could buy time, I would have it on auto-pay.

For over a year, my son, Joshua, expressed an interest in entrepreneurship on multiple occasions. At almost every community festival or vending event we attended, he would say, "Mom, I want my own business", "Mom, I want to sell comic books", or

"Mom, I want to make money and be rich". It was amazing to witness his motivation to start his own business. However, I know my child. He wasn't fully aware of the responsibilities that come with being an entrepreneur. On top of that, trouble always seems to come when you decide to start a new venture in life. My family and I have been hit with several hard blows in the last few years. I thought to myself, "with all that I'm going through, I don't have time to help him start a business. He doesn't understand the research, dedication, expenses, and sacrifices it takes to run a business." But that didn't stop Joshua. I should have named him "Persistence" because he never let go of his entrepreneurial desires.

It began with superhero comic books that he created. He used a black ink pen to illustrate, write, and mark the cover with a $1 price tag on loose leaf paper. Joshua took his comics to school to sell and to my surprise, a small number of his classmates bought them. As Christmas approached that year, he searched his closet for new/like-new toys and tried to sell them. In early 2018, he became inspired by his friend/Young Biz Kidz colleague, Mia, who sells delicious homemade cookies. He then wanted to sell homemade desserts. That's when I said, "Tanika, you're going to have to make time to help him bring together ideas to start a business. Don't let excuses stop greatness." I don't ever want to hold my children back from accomplishing their dreams, no matter how big or small.

It was mid-April 2018 when I had "the talk," explaining the basics of entrepreneurship to both of my children. I made it very clear that it is crucial to pray about everything and trust God for the answer. I wanted Joshua to understand that I truly supported his business aspirations and would guide him to the best of my ability. However, he had to learn the concept of responsibility and putting action to his entrepreneurial dreams. As I talked to them, I began to reflect on my own entrepreneurial efforts as a youth. I have a long history of hustlin'. When I was his age, I would use my allowance to buy Lisa Frank stationary kits and sell the items within the kit at school. I'd also buy packs of Now and Later candy from a local corner store and sell them as well. I only made a little profit from that, but a little profit was a big deal to my 11-year-old self. As the years passed, I went from selling Lisa Frank stationary and candy to custom name bracelets to "blinged-out" bandanas to braiding hair and installing sew-in weaves. I was serious about styling hair and studied the latest trends. This prompted me to practice on my own hair or dolls until I perfected the style. My clientele was pretty steady during my undergraduate years at college. Being a "kitchen beautician" relieved some financial burdens that I faced during and after college. I was able to overcome some of the financial challenges I was facing. After reflecting, I realized that Joshua was bitten by the same "entrepreneurial bug" that bit me at his age, and it was my duty to encourage him.

After "the talk", Joshua became more motivated and adamant about selling homemade desserts. The three of us brainstormed about different "treats" he could sell. That's when he suggested cake pops. A few years ago, I learned how to make cake pops and catered various social events for my co-workers, family, sorority sisters, and their associates. It was more of a hobby for me than a hustle, but once again, Joshua was persistent. "Mom those cake pops are good. You gotta sell them." I replied to my son, "I'm not selling them, you are. If you are serious about starting your own business, you're going to have to learn how to make them." Then my daughter said, "I want to help." Even though she's six, I thought it would be beneficial for her to learn about entrepreneurship, work ethic, and money management as well. During this brainstorming session, we prayed, chose products to sell, discussed prices, and how much time we wanted to invest in this endeavor. That's when "JZ's Sweets" was born.

When Joshua first learned how to make cake pops, he was very focused. I was in shock because he's typically a very playful child, but at that moment he was all about business. He studied the measurements of ingredients, brainstormed various flavor combinations, and attempted to develop new recipes. My daughter was just as serious as he was. On May 5, 2018, "JZ's Sweets" was launched and he sold his first batch of cake pops. Joshua made two batches of cake pops the night before so he could donate one batch to a local homeless shelter and sell the other. He took the initiative to visit several vendors at a festival we attended that day and talked about his business. A few people bought candy from him while others donated money for "business expenses". As launch day ended, you could taste the great joy that Joshua was feeling from his first day's profits. Since then, he's become more motivated to sell candy, obtain orders, and pass out business cards. Joshua and his sister tell everyone they meet about JZ's Sweets. They have given away samples and sold products at social events, parades, community centers, festivals, church, family gatherings, and more. He has been featured on a live TV segment for a local news station and has been asked to speak to students at elementary schools. All of this has helped JZ's Sweets gain exposure and show that it is very possible for children to become successful entrepreneurs.

In the short amount of time that JZ's Sweets has been opened, Joshua has developed character traits that are beneficial to its operation (time management, planning, design, research, and more). He's beginning to make cake pops independently from start to finish while constantly thinking of different cake batters and coatings to experiment with. He's becoming more capable of handling heat-related tasks with supervision. Joshua is driven to make sure that his cake pops are of high quality in every aspect (including taste, appearance, and packaging). He's hired his sister and best friend as assistants and is able to delegate appropriate tasks to them. Math wasn't always his favorite subject in school but now he sees how critical math is in operating a business. He enjoys attending classes or events that focus on financial literacy.

When Joshua initially discussed entrepreneurship, he mainly talked about "getting paid" and "being rich". Now he's understanding the concept of wealth, money management, setting financial goals, and building a legacy. We frequently discuss the importance of using the platform that JZ's Sweets has created to help others. Joshua has a special interest in helping children in foster care and those who are homeless. He believes that everyone (especially children) should have a safe and loving place to live. Because of his passion to help others, he has donated some of his profits to a local homeless shelter. In addition to this, he's inspired his friends to become entrepreneurs and has assisted them with drafting ideas for their own businesses. His sister is currently developing a business plan of her own.

Joshua is eager to expand JZ's Sweets. In the beginning, he mainly sold vanilla coated cake pops. He has now created seven other varieties of cake pops, candy-coated rice krispies treats and pretzels. He's more willing to sell different varieties of candy and is currently contemplating selling "JZ's Sweets" merchandise. Programs such as Young Biz Kidz and JA Biz Town has helped Joshua greatly in understanding the mechanisms of entrepreneurship. They have helped him to better understand the concepts of business expenses, inventory, profits, and banking. When we visit the grocery store, he tends to research and compare prices of candy and other desserts.

I consistently remind Joshua to remain humble and appreciative of every customer and supporter of JZ's Sweets. He has realized that he is not the only person in our city who sells candy and cake pops. When it's all said and done, people do not have to spend their money on JZ's Sweets. Therefore, Joshua has developed a great sense of appreciation. He has made it a habit to thank his supporters both personally and via social media. I believe that having a "thankful spirit" is a great character trait and valuable to his business.

At first, becoming a "Momager" seemed overwhelming. I didn't think I could handle everything I was experiencing in life along with this new role. I had to make the decision to not view it as a "job," but as a new journey for my family. I wanted my children to utilize this experience as a stepping stone for other opportunities. Additionally, I had to remind myself that my main role is to be supportive of Joshua and not overbearing. This experience is meant to be fun and something that he looks forward to working on. It is essential for him to take pride in owning his own business and strive towards taking it to another level.

Time management has become a priority in my life as a mother and Momager. My daily responsibilities as a mother would be in jeopardy of being neglected if I didn't prioritize and manage my time well. In our household, spirituality and education are essential. Prayer, homework, and other related tasks must be completed before other things. Also, I had to check myself to make sure that I was emotionally and mentally ready for the ride. I asked myself, "Tanika, can you support, encourage, and guide both of your children while helping Joshua build a new business?" Once I realized that I was capable of doing this, I learned a few gems as a newly appointed Momager:

• You have to ask yourself, "Is this something my child really wants to do or am I pushing him/her to do it for selfish reasons?" If this is your child's aspiration, develop a list of short-term and long-term goals together. As the Bible says, "Write the vision and make it plain." (Habakkuk 2:2).

• Invest in a planner especially for your child's business in order to keep track of vending events, shopping trips, social activities, to-do lists, etc.

- As the saying goes, "knowledge is power". Attend classes and seminars that focus on entrepreneurship, banking, and financial literacy. Take your child(ren) to classes that specialize in educating the youth in these areas. Schedule a meeting with the manager at your bank or credit union to gain more insight as well.

- Always be willing to learn. Recognize "teachable moments" for your child(ren). Network with other Momagers and small business owners. Inquire about how they got started and learn from their mistakes and successes.

- Realize that you don't know everything and it's ok to ask for help. It doesn't make you weak, it makes you wiser.

- Let your child be a child. Make entrepreneurship a fun experience for all of your children. Don't turn it into a chore that they may regret.

- "Just say no" to negativity. It will block your child(ren) and yourself from growing. Speak positivity into your lives. Surround yourself with a team of people who are supportive and can provide assistance when needed.

- Being a Momager has several positive attributes but it also adds more tasks to the daily duties of motherhood. Do not become weighed down by the demands and challenges of life. Check-in with yourself daily and regularly engage in healthy activities or hobbies that you enjoy. Make time to care for yourself so that you can effectively care for your child(ren) and successfully manage their business.

Life is filled with what we perceive as "impossibilities". There are many obstacles and challenges that we face which make it seem impossible to overcome in the natural realm. But a supernatural faith in God will allow one to overcome and conquer all that he/she may face. I often remind my children and myself of Matthew 19:26, especially when they become discouraged about school or a certain goal that they want to accomplish. Speak your requests into existence. Trust God's Word and watch your requests come to life. Put time and action towards your requests. Never stop believing in yourself and your children. No matter how busy you are, make time for yourself and your children. Do not become hindered by excuses. Make time to conquer the impossible.

For more information, please contact
JZ.Sweets@yahoo.com

Tamara M. Robinson
Entrepreneur, Real Estate Investor, Momager

Tamara M. Robinson is a successful business owner and real estate investor who partners with other CEOs, executives and entrepreneurs to empower the community through financial education. After spending a decade building her own businesses, Tamara knows what it takes to start your entrepreneurial journey and how to avoid many of the pitfalls of a new business owner.

Tamara is passionate about empowering people through entrepreneurship and financial literacy. Therefore, she has started coaching and consulting everyday people, transforming families, making a difference in the community. Tamara's true mission is to teach families how to leave a legacy, build wealth and become financially empowered.

Tamara holds a B.A. and MBA in business administration and has been featured in the local news as a "savvy business woman" when speaking about taking risks and buying real estate during the fall of the housing market.

I Am Tamara Robinson –Mom Boss

The Dream Chaser's Mom
by Tamara M Robinson, MBA

*"All our dreams can come true, if we have the
courage to pursue them." -Walt Disney*

Let's face it, we all have dreams; however, not all
of us dare to chase our dreams. I left my corporate job
9 years ago while pregnant with my first born, to
embark on my entrepreneurial journey. Courageous is
an understatement, I was fearless! I had significantly
more than a dollar and a dream. I had a master's
degree in business administration, and a 401k savings
plan fully matched by my employer. I soon
discovered, I was going to need more than money and
a graduate degree. I had courage, strength, patience, a
great work ethic, dedication, and faith, all the
characteristics no university or corporate career could
ever prepare me for. Oh, and did I mention that I
would need to like roller coasters, because
entrepreneurship comes with a lot of twists and turns?
I had to hold on tight and embrace the ride.

The Birth of a Business

On March 20, 2010, the first day of spring I gave
birth to a beautiful baby girl named Chase Mona'e
Robinson-Simmons. As a new mother and
entrepreneur, my priorities about time and money

drastically changed. Dad and I vowed we would not go back to a 9-5 job or a career that made someone else rich- entrepreneurship was now our new way of life. There was no turning back, we were all in. We decided to put our 401k savings together and invest in ourselves. We educated ourselves on how real estate investing was a way out of the rat race and could move us toward a path of financial freedom.

Have you ever seen those signs that say "we buy houses"? That was us! We put signs in every municipality around St Louis, Missouri. Chase was indeed my good luck charm! I took her everywhere; to prospect houses, title companies and closings where I signed contracts in one hand and held a bottle in the other. Entrepreneurship gave me the freedom to be both a mom and a business owner. Having the freedom to make decisions on how we use our own time has proven to be priceless.

I decided to homeschool Chase, from birth to age five. I created my own curriculum which included financial literacy and entrepreneurship. Learning about money at an early age was important to me, but also through playtime she learned the difference between a consumer and producer and I always encouraged her to be on the producer side. At age three, Chase was an early reader and could count money, however, was a late talker. So, most of our time was play based on switching roles and taking turns to be the business owner and the customer.

As Chase transitioned to preschool, we discovered that she had a speech and language delay. She could say words, read, and do skip counting and early math; however, she wasn't able to use her words and language to have a complete conversation with other children. Most of her preschool years were spent in speech/language therapy. *"Albert Einstein didn't talk till he was age 5"* her pediatrician kept telling us. Ironically, Chase also did not fully talk until the age of 5. As frustrating as it was for her socially, she continued learning math and was very interested in coins, dollars and their value. Her speech and language delay never kept her from learning. Socially she was struggling, however, she was always academically ahead grade levels. Since I was an entrepreneur, I had the freedom of my time to take her to speech and language therapy 4- 5 times per week, preschool half of day, and still create a tailored curriculum for Chase.

Once school started full time for her, she became interested in starting a business, real estate, and buying stocks because those were our family discussions at dinner time together. We spoke candidly about money, the different ways money can grow, how to buy ugly houses and make them look pretty and rent them for cash flow. These financial terms had become just as easy as learning the alphabet to her. When there was an opportunity to buy a rental investment property, she would come along and become very intrigued about the process. This is really a critical factor in changing your child's mindset about being a producer and a problem solver because that is exactly what an entrepreneur is. Our family activity time consists of games like cash flow, Monopoly, and chess. These games are not only great learning tools and fun, but they also help her with the necessary skills and techniques to become a great thinker and problem solver, therefore a successful entrepreneur.

Chasing a Dream

Chase's entrepreneurial journey started by her one day asking "why don't they teach kids at school to start their own businesses?" I didn't have a definite child appropriate answer, so I replied to her "I am not sure, but it is my life mission to change that, you just chase your dreams, do whatever it is you want, work hard and be dedicated in all you do, your dreams are awaiting you."

This soon became our daily affirmation, we would wake up in the morning, look ourselves in the mirror and affirm to our mirrored image what we wanted to be that day. Chase would say, "I am smart, bold, brave, and I can do anything." These affirmations are key to building your children's confidence, and it is necessary to do before you go out into a world that will tell you "you can't do this, and you can't do that." I often call these people, dream snatchers.

One day Chase said, "I am a dream chaser!" She expressed to me she wanted to start a club with her friends and teach them about financial literacy and entrepreneurship. I told her it was an extraordinary idea so, we put a plan together. We made flyers and she recruited seven members all on her own. The views and creativity from her were astonishing, I was just there to implement her vision. She called her club, The Dream Chasers! She has also saved all her coins and dollar bills and purchased three candy vending machines. All the proceeds go to The Dream Chasers club to teach kids financial literacy and entrepreneurship.

Chase has willingly stepped into the world of an entrepreneur, and it is an amazing journey. She has sacrificed an entire year of playing sports to focus on her club and business. I have learned that you must be organized by keeping a schedule and creating balance. Chase uses a planner for school, violin, piano lessons and also for her business. Staying aware of what's coming, we can schedule the time to meet deadlines. The same strategies parents use to balance their kids' busy sports, and athletic schedules can be used when your child is an entrepreneur. It's a real challenge to do a business, sports, music and classes; therefore, Chase is sacrificing her love for sports at the moment to focus on her business goals. When you make hard choices, you are forcing yourself to take a risk and take action.

Lastly, it is imperative that our children are taught delayed gratification. They must understand the concept of discipline and self-control and know that success does not happen overnight. If we put in the hard work now, teaching them to wait to reap the rewards, our children will learn the important concepts of patience and discipline. The road less traveled is often the road where there are great opportunities and many awards. I found that surrounding our daughter with like-minded children, in organizations like Young Biz Kidz and The Dream Chasers Financial Lit Club has opened the doors for endless possibilities. Therefore, she does not have to travel on this road alone. She will chase her dreams, aim high and inspire others along her journey. As Harriet Tubman once said, "Every great dream begins with a dreamer."

"Always remember you have within you the strength, the patience, and the passion that guides you to reach for the stars and change the world."

For more information contact:
Email: tamararobinson.consulting@gmail.com
Office: (415) 903-0052
FB: tamararobinsonconsultingllc
IG: tamararobinson.consulting

Sauywanna Davis
Educator, Technology Specialist, Momager

Ms. Sauywanna Davis is a single mother of one son named Kaionta R. Dabney. She works in education and information technology. Her dedication to teaching, education and professional experience, make her a successful momager and entrepreneur.

In the course of her academic career, Sauywanna received a B.A. in Business Administration, B.S. in Management Information Systems, M.A. in Computer Resource & Information Management and a Teacher Certification. All of her exposure, be it from college classes, seminars or workshops, spilled over and combined with her creativity. The result became a design to teach students basic math skills through the craft of making keychains. The project was well received by both students and staff alike and served as the inspiration for her son's entrepreneurial endeavors.

Through the fun craft of making keychains, Kaionta discovered he too could share the concepts which teach fractions, percentages, decimals, geometry and measurements. Thus, his business Keychain Karnival was created.

Sauywanna and Kaionta's next goal is to host workshops for hands-on demonstrations while using mathematical concepts to create beaded keychains. This creates a platform for Kaionta to author a book which correlates with lessons taught in the workshop.

When described by her close friends Sauywanna is often regarded as humble, willing to share skills to teach others, one who assists with technology endeavors, a researcher, passionate about youth camps and giving.

I Am Sauywanna Davis –Mom Boss

How It All Began,
Math Concepts Thru Keychain Karnival
by Ms. Sauywanna Davis

"For I know the plans I have for you plans to prosper you and not to harm you, plans to give you hope and a future." - Jeremiah 29:11 (NIV)

Hello to all my parents, my name is Ms. Sauywanna Davis. I am a single mother of a fifteen-year-old son, Kaionta R. Dabney. My background spans across several industries, but my credentials attest to the following: I hold a B.A. in Business Administration, B.S.in Management Information Systems, M.A. in Computer Resource & Information Management and Education.

Strength in Numbers

I was working in the IT field at a casino, until I was released from my duties on January 1, 2018. I thought, now that I have this time off, I can assist my son with his keychain business that literally stemmed from my lesson plans in my math class. We all know, without math, the world would not exist nor can we as individuals function daily. During my time as an educator in mathematics, students struggled with basic skills of decimals, fractions, percentages, geometry, and measurements.

One day, all of a sudden, a clear vision was revealed to me to create a project called, "Math Discovery thru Keychains." I purchased a keychain kit from Walmart and presented it to my students. After the students created their keychain of choice, I began my math lesson. We discussed the total number of beads used, colors and the measurement of a satin cord. With the data provided, I demonstrated how to:

- Calculate the fraction of colors (numerator-colors/denominator-total beads used)
- Convert the fraction into a percent (using long division) & obtain a decimal answer
- Identify geometrical angles and degrees' in their keychain
- Identify the required measurements & convert to inches or feet

When my first class completed this project, they were so exhilarated about the learning process, they began to showcase their craft to other students and staff, causing an amazing amount of interest. Needless to say, armed with newfound enthusiasm, I expanded my teaching platform, providing this project to all my classes. Some of my co-workers sent their eager students to my class to learn these new concepts that were quickly becoming very popular in the school.

The kits from Walmart did not meet the demand for this learning technique. I soon realized, further research for material in bulk quantities would be my best option to keep up with the request for the Keychain Project. During my research, I found wholesalers for the hair beads (Pony Beads), satin chord and key rings (Hobby Lobby). As my students became more knowledgeable, they're creativity intensified. They began wanting more challenges, using other characters, designs or objects to create using the hair beads. Overwhelmed with the various beaded keychain designs, we created a binder that showed, beginning, intermediate, and advanced levels. All my students were elated at what we created. Now you're probably thinking, "How does this relate to my son's entrepreneurship?"

Well, this part involves my mother, who's task was picking up my son from school. Kaionta and my mother would come sit in my class after my students left for the day but this day would prove to be amazing and different. Kaionta witnessed the students' demonstrations on the chalkboard which covered the components of the lesson that held the key to the Keychain project and moreover, the Keychain Karnival. Kaionta was immediately fascinated by what he had seen, prompting him to declare, "Mom I want to make a keychain too!" My mom quickly added, "Don't leave me out!" At the time, my son was only 6 years old but can you guess what I did? I purchased them both a keychain kit. From that point on, in my son's free time, he wanted to see what keychains he could make.

I started introducing to him the basic math concepts I covered with my students. He was only in first grade at the time so, he didn't fully grasp my project. As he continued to evolve in age, those concepts would be revisited and performed more frequently, breaking through the barriers of understanding. In addition, my mom would awake in the morning making keychains, sitting for hours at the table challenging herself on all three levels.

My son asked me one day if I could buy him some toys because he didn't have any money. I suggested to him, "How about we try to sell these keychains you designed." The mentor organization he is affiliated with sponsored a breakfast and allowed vendors to sell their products. We asked if Kaionta could participate as a vendor. Kaionta set up his booth for all the visitors to see his hard work. At the age of 6 years old, Kaionta made over $75 while demonstrating the math concepts with keychains he had made with the help of my mother and me.

What 6 year old wouldn't be animated about making money like that? To him that was gold. He used the concept he was taught early on, (learning math with keychains) to create a lucrative opportunity. I asked if he thought about transforming this into a business, teaching math through craft to make money. "Ok Mom, let's do this," he replied and a business was born. We began to brainstorm business names, something catchy for children and an inquiry for adults. The name was established, Keychain Karnival and the slogan: ***"Handmade beaded keychains of various designs, characters and more. Flying high as a kid entrepreneur."***

As this was the beginning of entrepreneurship for both of us, we were excited. We started designing more keychains for his inventory to demonstrate math concepts for the next event. To expound on the concepts of the keychains, I shared with my son he needed a poster board. The poster board displayed how some of the keychains represent a connection to African American's first inventions. He said, "How can we do that mom?" I asked him to name some of the keychains. He made ice cream cones, hearts, footballs, and a clock, just to name a few. I was able to show my son how the history of African American inventors tied into the keychain concepts as an addition to math:

> • Ice Cream – Augustus Jackson was renowned for many popular ice cream recipes and became one of the wealthiest African Americans in Philadelphia during his time

• Heart – Dr. Daniel Hale Williams was the 1ˢᵗ to perform open heart surgery.

• Football – Charles W. Follis was announced the first African American professional NFL player.
• Clock - Benjamin Banneker developed America's first fully operative clock.

On Kaionta's display board he noted the cost and pictures of keychains representing African Americans who paved the way in our culture. In addition, it showed how the inventions contributed to a more productive society and gave a brief synopsis about the inventors. What Kaionta decided to do was to educate himself on these great inventors by researching their biographies. From there, he would be able to elaborate his findings to the community as they visited events. His first big event was to be a vendor at the Kwanza Expo hosted by Better Family Life, held at Cardinal Ritter High School. Kaionta was the youngest entrepreneur at the age of 7-years-old. As people would stop by his booth, he would speak about his business, how to perform calculations and what inspired him with this concept/product. He told the history of some of the most successful people on his display. Many were so impressed by this 7 year old, several people simply donated money for his public speaking skills and deliverance on African American history!

As Kaionta's business began to grow with success as a young entrepreneur, we added business cards, a banner, postcards, and a photo table display to his marketing profile. Seeing how successful Keychain Karnival has become, as a mom, I had to make sure my son could continue to be a child and not get lost in the experience. He would only participate as a vendor during the school year 2-3 times at local craft events and of course, at such a young age, he was not able to create/produce inventory by himself. As with most child entrepreneurs, had the support of family - my mom and myself.

Over the past 7 years, Kaionta has been showcasing his business, developing an articulate speaking tone and demonstrating support to other vendors. Although he always had his business cards ready (never miss an opportunity to market) when he visited other booths, he would generally make a purchase of their products.

Kaionta has evolved in delivering concepts about his business, how it helps other kids to learn math and has picked up some valuable history lessons himself as an added bonus. One of Kaionta's special request came for a 6-year-old girl's birthday party. The mom visited Kaionta at a Kid Expo event where he was vending. The customer mentioned her daughter's birthday theme was a bubble gum machine. She then requested 5 bubble gum keychains for the party. He had never made a bubble gum machine keychain before, so he was excited about the challenge. Kaionta was able to view a bubble gum machine and fulfill the order for the birthday party. This opportunity was a new level for Keychain Karnival and a good marketing tool that could be shared by the party girl's mom to friends and family.

To assist with marketing Kaionta's business, he has started composing his book called, "Math Discovery Thru Keychain Karnival." The book will be used to host workshops with hands-on demonstrations creating keychains. Children will gain an understanding of those basic math skills discussed earlier. Kaionta plans to visit schools to speak with students and introduce them to his math concepts through a fun, engaging and creative way. In addition, he will share his entrepreneurial journey telling why and how he is the young man, he is today.

As a first-time single mom, I am very blessed that God used my math class and me to be an inspiration to my son's entrepreneurial spirit. Had the concepts never been revealed to me, my son would not know the connection between math, history, and keychains. These 7 years have been exploratory for all of us. Networking and meeting new people who are inspired by what he has accomplished at such a young age is very rewarding for us both.

Not only is this a business, but these wonderful keychains are now a vehicle that assists in the transfer of knowledge, while teaching skills relative to one of the most profound subjects that society has to use in everyday life. Occasionally, I remind my son to acknowledge who has made this happen for him. It was not me, but God, who planted a vision in me to share with him. Now, he can continue to spread the knowledge to other children, while traveling within his entrepreneurial territory. I can't think of a better way for children to learn math, than by the teachings of another child, through the simplicity of craft. Kaionta is blessed with an opportunity to share his story with many others. I pray that he and every other young aspiring entrepreneur never forgets who carries them, who has laid the foundation and who stands behind them in support.

To all my parents, what good is a child's talent if it's not being tapped into? As parents, you should recognize their interest, skills, talents, and abilities then encourage them to prepare for the world. Once defined, begin to pray for your village, patience, guidance, support, balance, research, and development. Arrange networking opportunities with supporters who have traveled this exploratory journey. Participate in local events to start your child on his/her entrepreneurial adventure. Over time, you will help them discover patience, understanding, growth and development is key to you and your child. Always and never forget, your child is a kid and should not be deprived of conducting themselves as a kid, as you once were at their age! Remember, it is a disgrace to let that talent go to waste.

"The LORD makes firm the steps of the one who delights in him; though he may stumble, he will not fall, for the LORD upholds him with his hand." -Psalm 37:23-24 (N

Should you have any questions, I can be reached at:
swaunnie01@gmail.com

Aunkule Benford-Campbell
Entrepreneur, Beauty Consultant, Momager

Aunkule Benford-Campbell efforts to use her personal and professional life lessons to positively impact those she encounters daily. Organization, customer service and establishing a foundation of loving kindness are some of her strongest qualities. Hailing from a strong family unit where entrepreneurialism was both instilled and necessary, she learned early that having a business mindset would prepare her in all aspects of life. Later she would draw from her work in retail management, education, and beauty industries, to assist her in managing her home and business. Her greatest desire is to use her experiences and skills to teach and inspire her children.

Aunkule owns a beauty consultant business where she specializes in lash and hair extensions. She takes pride in helping her clients achieve their most authentic and personal beauty brand image.

Aunkule holds a B.A. in Elementary Education from Harris-Stowe State University and is married with three wonderful daughters.

I am Aunkule Benford-Campbell – Mom Boss

Parenting in an Entrepreneurial Household
by Aunkule Benford-Campbell

"Success is the sum of small efforts, repeated day in and day out." – Robert Collier

An entrepreneurial spirit can be instilled and nurtured in young people. As parents, it is our responsibility to help foster good practices, create meaningful experiences, and celebrate the natural talents of our children. Now, if you have had the opportunity to spend any significant time with children, you know that even the best-made plans are not always going to create the outcomes desired. Even so, having no plan will never get you to the place you want to be.

As a mom of three children with very different personalities, gifts, and energy levels; I realize that not everything works for every child. However, over the years, I have been able to reflect on the consistent themes that have worked for my family and me as I instill business practices in all aspects of our lives. I hope that you find these take-aways helpful as you begin (or continue) inspiring the young people in your life to become confident, driven, organized and financially independent business-minded people.

Reflecting on how I first became aware of business basics, I remember lessons from my parents who were my first teachers. Growing up in a large family with a structured and loving foundation, I now realize how many aspects of ethical business practices were modeled by my parents. My father was a very respected and respectful man showing me how to treat others. He reminded me to be kind and to follow through on my commitments. My mother showed me how to organize spaces and fiscally manage through tough times. She taught me that everything had a place and function and that attention to detail saved time and money. At the time, I didn't appreciate how these simple concepts would set the foundation for my success, but in retrospect, I am very thankful for their direction. I was introduced to a way of thinking that sparked creativity, dedication, and follow-through. I would use their simple wisdom as the foundation for creating and managing my personal and professional lives.

Years later I began a career in retail management and was formally introduced to terms, theories and concepts of good business practice. The company I worked for gave me access to expensive professional development. I coupled that with a formal college education and took a few courses which, highlighted leadership and management. I was confident in what my formal education afforded me. Ironically, after much reflection, I determined that many of the philosophies of successful business management were identical to the ones I learned by watching my hard-working, informally trained parents. It became apparent that great business minds can learn from anyone, anywhere and that by merely modeling successful practices at home, the youngest of children could gain an understanding of the basic concepts behind highly successful habits. This would soon be my primary mission.

So, with all of that great information, retail management experience, time as a professional school teacher, wife of an entrepreneur, and now the owner of a home-based business, one would think I would have absolutely no trouble inspiring a love for business in my children – right? Wrong! As much as I'd like to make my three girls "absolute identical replicas of myself," it just didn't happen. I somehow ended up with three young ladies who have their own minds, personalities, and talents – who knew? The things that inspire me or that give me absolute joy may or may not be the motivating factors for my daughters. While I did end up with three very business-focused children, the path to engaging them was unique to their ages, talents and individual choices.

The consistent themes which help me as a mom, are the ones I share most and I hope are helpful to other "Parent-preneurs" (you know we must always support one another!) With each of the concepts I want to teach my children, I ask myself, "what does this look like, sound like and how am I modeling it?" This structure helps both my girls and me. It is especially important also to acknowledge and celebrate when my children learn something new or positively demonstrate beneficial outcomes. As the first investor in your child's life and small business, it is a good idea to establish an informal learning plan which will help them in all aspects of their lives.

The following are topics that have helped me develop and support the business of my daughters while also encouraging me to be a better parent.

1. Teach Organization

An organized life fosters a coordinated mind and supports a coordinated plan.

I would love to say that my children absolutely adore keeping an organized room, voluntarily take responsibility for putting things back into place and never complains while doing it. However, that is most certainly not the case for my kids or even my husband! Most people would be overjoyed to have a maid, nanny or mom be responsible for keeping spaces neat. While that may be our initial desire, there is power in personally maintaining order in your business and personal life that benefits everyone involved.

71

With my home-based business and down-sized space, it is critical to have organizational systems in place that allow for the best practice of "touching it once" and executing tasks most efficiently.

An organized home

- *What does it look like?*

All items have designated and (where appropriate) labeled places in our home. Keeping tidy spaces allows you to reduce the time and fiscal resources by not needing to find or replace lost items.

- *What does it sound like?*

"Hey mom, I'm doing my laundry, and I saw that we are getting low on detergent pods. I looked in the replenishing bin to refill them, but there was none there. I'll add detergent pods to the shopping list since we are down to our last five pods."

The example is indicative of systems in place to store, replenish, and repurchase supplies in the household.

Organize your time

- *What does it look like?*

Each child is assigned a task or role to maintain the family calendar. This helps to remind each family member of critical upcoming events so that we can plan accordingly. Some duties include: marking off previous days, noting when school is not in session, indicating family times, holidays and special events; and using color-coded markers for each child's schedule.

- *What does it sound like?*
To my pre-teen, I may say, "Today let's add your school concerts, conferences, and field trips to the calendar. Be sure to use orange to highlight your events, and I'll use green to indicate your younger sister's."

To my 6- year old, I might add, "Go ahead and mark off the previous day that has passed and put a check on the events we attended."

Here we see examples of age and developmentally appropriate tasks being considered for each child. When my girls manage their spaces and times without being told, they are immediately acknowledged and celebrated. I am sure to point out precisely what I appreciated about their performance. I encourage discussions with their input on how they are benefiting from the organized environment we are all helping to maintain. We discuss how the concepts are necessary for both realms of running a home and running a business. Organization is a crucial concept that all young business minds should not only have, but also embrace.

2. Create Opportunities

Most of the time opportunities don't just happen...they must be sought.

It is ever present, for me, the need to create opportunities to develop, or further enhance, my daughters' business skills. I take time to discuss areas of their businesses we want to grow. Being in programs that support these efforts and nurture their creativity is a must.

- *What does it look like?*

We made sure our girls were enrolled in programs like Young Biz Kidz (YBK) for entrepreneurial youth and are able to attend expos and market place events which are selling platforms for young entrepreneurs.

- *What does it sound like?*

My retail experience prepared me for modeling ways to engage potential customers with words and corresponding actions that generate sales.

"Hi. Have you had a chance to smell our candles today?" – (said while extending an open candle jar for them to smell and hold).

Allow your young ones to shadow a skilled performer when possible.

I remember a time when my middle child and I were at a market place event with other young entrepreneurs to allow her to promote her business and sell items. We set up a table of different toys, gadgets and hand-crafted items for her business. This daughter, unlike her siblings, tends to be introverted and I fully expected that my demonstration of skills and customer service engagement would be rather extensive. In other words, I believed she would not be eager to speak to strangers and would focus on other tasks when customers arrived. I resolved that I would be the face and voice of her business that day. So as people began to come, I fell into sales mode. After a short time, however, I noticed that at the other end of the table, my child was actually mimicking my customer engagement approach to potential customers.

Later when we were recapping the day's events, I asked my daughter what made her jump in on the effort to generate sales. She shared with me that she reasoned within herself, "Hey...this is MY business and it is only right that I should have to speak to people too."

I was so happy and proud at this moment for several reasons. First, my intention in involving my daughter with the business

*program was to sharpen her natural skills
and help her develop her business plan. I
secondly wanted to create various
opportunities for her to promote her items
and be rewarded by providing a product that
others wanted. What I had hoped most of all
was that she would gain opportunities to
express herself clearly and develop a comfort
with engaging others in dialogue – something
that did not come naturally or easily for her.*

*I was also thrilled to hear that she was
willing to overcome her discomfort of
interacting with others to meet what proved
to be greater – a need for her to do her part
in the outcome of her own business.*

3. Develop Character

*The best contribution to the world is a loving and
kind human being.*

When I look at some of the most financially
successful individuals in life, I am not always
impressed by their personalities. Whether they are
self-made or inherited their wealth, people tend to
remember how well they or their companies treated
people. Raising successful children for me means
developing young people who have a spirit that I am
proud of, and whose contributions to our society are
more than financial. Developing a child's character

is just as important (if not more) as developing other skills to make them highly successful.

Everyone is aware that a negative attitude affects everyone on the team. How you respond to uncomfortable situations or failure can really showcase a person's character.

• *What does it look like?*
I intend to help guide my daughters' response to negativity, pride, anger, sadness and other emotions that we often encounter in life. It is beneficial to provide them with tools and strategies to assist them when navigating situations in hopes of a positive outcome.

• *What does it sound like?*
At those times when the girls disagree with their sibling, and one child uses their size or intelligence to push their will, I often focus my response in a way that directs their thinking to consider how their behavior hurts not only others but also themselves. I have often modeled for the girls what it sounds like to state and acknowledge their wrong course of action and what it seems like to say and acknowledge a path that leads to the upbuilding of one another. I ask them to demonstrate the model while making direct eye contact with one another.

This example of modeling shows how to treat each other and continue the dialogue on more appropriate ways to respond. Consider additional character traits including follow-through and duty.

I remember when my daughter was invited to a theme park with friends the day before a youth entrepreneurial event. We still had several to-dos on our checklist and hand-crafted products to make. She really, really wanted to attend the event, and it would surely be a great deal of fun. As an investor in her business, I was entirely in my rights to give my opinion, but I refrained. This was HER business. She thought about it for a while and decided that although she would LOVE to meet with her friends, it wouldn't be fair to leave all of the work for everyone else to do. This helped me to see her growth and maturity. I learned how she valued teamwork and the extent of her work ethic. It was at that time that she set the tone for what she would do for her business and set an example of how others should be willing to do the same. I appreciated that she acknowledged her role herself.

We decided that after the event was over, we would reward ourselves with a celebration – possibly a trip to the theme park.

4. Invest and Execute

After you've researched, prepared and prayed, it's time to do the work.

As parents, we must invest in our children and their dreams. When my daughters wanted to try their hands at being young entrepreneurs, my husband and I spent our time, money and resources to support them. After guiding them through the initial business steps, we began to step back, just enough, to allow them to be the leaders of their endeavors and business ventures.

- *What does it look like?*

In business, as it is also in the home, job descriptions or roles are outlined and defined so that all members may clearly understand how or what they contribute to the collective. My husband and I often reiterated to our daughters what areas of their lives they were expected to manage. They had assigned chores and responsibilities and we made sure they knew the business ventures they began were not ours to maintain, promote or push -- we were merely co-partners. It is essential, even though sometimes difficult, to let our children drive their businesses and experience the growth that comes with both the ups and downs. We were confident in the foundation of support that we had given our girls. It was now time to allow them to put it all to use for what we had empowered them to do-- be successful executers. They had what it took to do their jobs. Now they had to do it.

- *What does it sound like?*

My youngest daughter is responsible for storing certain goods purchased from the grocery store. These include snacks, drinks, tissues, and paper products. This is a routine repeated three to five times monthly. As items are unloaded from grocery bags, she begins sorting and placing them in their corresponding areas. My six-year-old travels from the pantry to the linen closet unpacking boxes, removing plastic wrappings, storing items in labeled bins, etc. She discards all the waste before checking in to assist further. She knows what to do, how to do it successfully, and feels good about doing her share.

> *Before entering middle school, I decided to have my eleven-year-old do a summer internship with me as a personal assistant. Some of her duties consisted of reading, communicating and scheduling incoming appointment requests and to then document dates, times and services on my work schedule. I hoped that she would experience the independence and partnership of managing her personal calendar, my business schedule and family time.*

> *Her daily personal agenda consisted of three house chores, three academic focuses, and*

2-3 personal activity choices. My daughter was able to independently choose from an agreed upon list of tasks on each category. We discussed her to-do list daily, Monday – Friday, to ensure that it fits the need of each day.

With her assistance in filling in my calendar, she had a first-hand look at my efforts to balance work, personal and family time. She was able to note how we incorporated getting business supplies, completed household errand runs, and how to prioritize and facilitate the daily plan. We were able to plug in family activities and downtime on the calendar, and schedule clients around these dates and times.

This internship allowed my daughter to gain perspective on the daily ins and outs of planning, preparing, and operation of running a business. I believe that these skills would be needed to manage the busy schedule she would have in middle school. She would soon embark on a world of choosing courses, 2-minute classroom changes, lockers, and locker combinations, crowded halls and traveling from one side of a three-story building to the next.

Regardless of formal or informal training, you too can foster an entrepreneurial spirit in your child. Lay a foundation of a business mindset by modeling and demonstrating the benefits of your strengths or best practices. Consider ways to use and incorporate organizational skills in their daily lives and seek out opportunities to surround them with business minded people or programs. Remember to build the character of your young one as business is most often conducted between people. Lastly, as they have been strengthened with knowledge, strategies, and experiences, allow them to do the work they've been equipped to do. The lessons learned while doing their part and taking ownership at this age will stay with them forever.

For more information contact:
Aunkule Benford Campbell
aunkule@att.net

Latrice C. Floyd
Educator, Visual Artist, Momager

Latrice C. Floyd is a pre-school educator, mother of 4, momager of 2 and owner/self taught artist of Destined 2 Paint LLC. She provides her customers with adult/child paint parties, custom canvases/portraits, face painting and live painting.

Latrice studied art at Southeast Missouri State University for a year but received her Bachelor's degree in Child Development.

One of Latrice's proudest moments as a local artist was being featured on Fox 2 news painting live. Seeing this accomplishment, amongst others, inspired her two youngest children, Reagan (Creations by Cheyenne) & Logan (Little Monsters Art) to become members of Young Biz Kidz and begin their journey into financial literacy and entrepreneurship as visual artists.

Her mission is to ensure that she continues to pour creativity and positivity into her children so they are aware that with hard work, faith and dedication you can achieve anything you put your mind to.

I Am Latrice Floyd –Mom Boss

One Mom + Two Kidpreneurs
by Latrice C. Floyd

How do you do it, girl!!??

To be or not to be a momager, that is the question! Right? I know what you're thinking. "How in the world do you balance life, work, entrepreneurship, and still have time for yourself, and make sure your feet look good?" Well, I've concluded that there is definitely a higher power helping me out down here or else I would've quit a long time ago. Being a momager is very challenging but it is also very rewarding at the same time and it can be done!!

When I decided to take on the role of being a momager I knew that I was going to have to surround myself with like-minded moms to keep me focused and grounded. My experience has taught me that even though, it's a lot of work and rough days, there are also a ton of great days!! I've had to learn to balance everything around me so that I could effectively manage everyone and not lose myself in the process.

Drawing on what you love to do

Ok, so let me give you a little background about myself. Growing up I always told my mom that I couldn't draw but still she always encouraged me to keep going and to never say "can't." She also enrolled me into an art program one summer where I learned a lot of new art techniques. I remember the first time in third grade one of my pieces I drew/painted from art class was put on display. I was ecstatic!! That is when I knew that my mother was right and that giving up wasn't an option. I kept on drawing right through middle school and into high school where I entered a drawing contest and won for the book cover of our yearbook.

During my high school Freshman year, we lost a classmate and I decided to test my skills and draw a portrait of her to hang in my room. Even though it wasn't my intent, I received a lot of good reviews on the portrait and I decided to continue to draw portraits of some of my favorite singers back then including Shazaam.

Heading into my college experience as an undergraduate, I majored in art for my first year which helped steer me into my first entrepreneurial role as a student! I customized hoodies, T-shirt's and hand bags for Greek-lettered organizations, fellow classmates and family members.

Today, I am the owner and artist of Destined 2 Paint LLC where I provide customers with custom canvases, portraits, live painting, face painting and paint parties! I am a single mom of 3 boys and 1 girl, ages 13, 12, 9 and 8 (two of which are kidpreneurs) and a full-time preschool teacher for YWCA Head Start. I am also a member of Raising a Mogul Community which is a support group for parents raising young moguls. On top of being a momager, I'm also a dance/basketball mom and soon to be a soccer mom. My 2 oldest sons play basketball for their school and my daughter dances for Outstanding Starz Majorette Team...but yes, I get my sleep!

"Every child is an artist. The problem is how to remain an artist once we grow up," -Pablo Picasso

The Birth of Destined 2 Paint!!

Okay so now that I've given you some background on how I became a business owner, let me be transparent for a second and let you know how I lost my way and started on my art journey again. Well, roughly 4 years ago I was unemployed, homeless and had recently just released myself from a very toxic relationship which sent me into a deep depression. I became very distant from friends and family and just wanted to be there for my kids. Fast forward to the summer of 2016- my good friend and former boss Ms. E, asked me to create a piece for her grandson's birthday. Well, I pulled myself together, began working a part-time job, picked up a few supplies, started and finished the commission for her, and I've been painting ever since! I had no intention of even picking up a brush again despite everyone telling me that I needed to get back to it. My unfortunate circumstances led me back to my God-given gift, and that is when Destined 2 Paint was created!!

"When you get, give…when you learn, teach." - Dr. Maya Angelou

Here comes Creations by Cheyenne!!

Painting is an outlet, and eventually when I was presented with the opportunity to showcase my skills I began painting live at different open mics, barbershops, women empowerment events and more around St. Louis. Whenever I had the opportunity, I would take my children to every kid-friendly event I was showcasing so that they could see I was not only working but I was doing something that I loved to do. Shortly after attending several events, my children started to get the "art bug," especially my daughter Reagan. Now Reagan has always been able to color and even at an early age she was very good. I have my mother to thank for that as well. At NaNa's house there was always a new coloring book and a fresh box of crayons waiting on my children, even to this day! I can still hear Reagan's daycare teacher say, "she has always been able to color, and I would just stare at her pictures and knew she was going to do something with art." I started off letting her just randomly paint at home, taking her own supply runs, then I started taking her to events with me so she could get a full glimpse of what mommy does when I'm vending or talking with customers. Well, that's pretty much all it took for her to say "Mama, I want to paint and make some money too!" From that Creations by Cheyenne was born.

Reagan's first showcase was in June of 2017 at a pop-up shop held by BeBold Cosmetics. She learned how to set up and price her artwork which is something that is still tricky for me at times. She had such a great time I decided to keep her going and have her paint live at the next upcoming event I signed up for. The Juneteenth Festival hosted by Young Voices with Action at Trojan Park in Wellston, MO was it. Here Reagan was able to let her hair down, feel the vibes and create whatever her little heart desired!

This was also around the time that I started her social media pages on Instagram and Facebook to get the word out that I was raising a kidpreneur who was a visual artist. After that, Reagan had 3 more events she participated in July and ended with Consciousfest in September.

In November 2017, Reagan was given the opportunity to paint live again and showcase with me at the Real Black Friday. She had such a great time there and actually ended up selling out of her paintings!! That was such a big moment for her, so she decided to buy herself, and a new friend kidpreneur, lunch after a long day of working hard!

In January 2018 we met Ms. Arriel Bivens-Biggs, founder of Young Biz Kidz at the 2nd annual Back 2 the Books, hosted by Ms. Tiffany Nelson, owner of Totes for Tomorrow. We were introduced to her and were instantly filled with excitement to have the opportunity to be a part of such a great organization! We had no idea the impact that Arriel was going to have on us and our entrepreneur journey! To add on to the excitement, we were also introduced to Mr. Tony Davis, owner of Made Moguls in St. Louis. He presented us with the opportunity for Reagan to receive a nomination for an award in the category of Youth Entrepreneur. This was very overwhelming for Reagan to grasp in the beginning because she was, and still is camera shy at times, but luckily she did not have to give a speech that night, and she was quite okay with that!

In April 2018, Reagan was asked to face paint for the Week of the Young Child at Kidz of Joy Development Center which is also something that she loves to do! In June of 2018, Reagan was able to be a part of her very first Young Biz Kid workshop at Midwest Bank as an official member. Soon after in July, she received an opportunity to instruct her first paint party for her YBK friend Skai who is the owner of her non-profit Skai Cares. Skai Cares provides those who are less fortunate with everyday essentials like gloves, hats, care packages, etc.

In June, Reagan also attended her first YBK workshop. The workshops consist of teaching financial literacy to parents and their future moguls. Being a member of Young Biz Kidz opens doors of opportunities for all of the kid bosses and also keeps us boss moms on our toes. Like I've said before, it is imperative to maintain a circle of like-minded individuals around you to ensure that you don't lose sight of your vision and goals and to promote growth within the business world. Young Biz Kidz also strives to teach our youth that entrepreneurship is an option. In addition, managing money and speaking in public about your brand is very relevant to a successful business. Financial literacy wasn't really a big thing in my household growing up nor was entrepreneurship. For me, this is an opportunity to "break the cycle" and ensure that my children are aware of entrepreneurship and have a financial education. Balance is vital and although I am still striving to get us to a place of economic freedom, I have come up with some ideas to make sure that my kids can get some one-on-one time with me. We are so glad to be a part of such an inspirational organization here in our home town St. Louis.

"Train up a child in the way he should go, even when he is old, he shall not depart from it." - Proverbs 22:6

Little Monster's Art speaks out!!

Alright! Are you ready to learn about my 2nd kidpreneur - Logan? Okay so, of course, after seeing his big sister going to events with me and coming back with her own money and sometimes a souvenir she bought herself for reaching her goal, he wanted to get on board. Well, I couldn't tell him no because that wouldn't be fair to let his talents and drive go to waste. I knew it would be even more challenging to manage my company and two more, but I was determined to make it happen! In the midst of this, my 2 oldest children also began going to the workshops taught by Mr. Cortez Springer (financial health mentor), but are still deciding on what they want to do as far as entrepreneurship goes.

With Logan being the youngest of four children, he has no problem saying what he wants and getting out there and hustling for himself. He didn't have a name for his brand though, so this is when I turned to my super creative and supportive friend Camron and asked him what he thought Logan's business name should be. Without any hesitation he suggested, "Little Monster's Art" since he's always calling Logan a little monster anyway. It just fit!! Now that we had his name it was time to really put in some work to build his brand.

Before Logan even joined YBK I would have people coming up to me at different events saying, "I met your son and he sold me one of his drawings for a $1." I was in total shock and had no idea that he too wanted to showcase his art and make money and once I finally told him that he was now an official member of YBK his creativity took off. Even though they have two different styles of artwork, he and Reagan collaborated and sold their art together at another marketplace for Midwest Bank in August 2018. This helped them learn to work together on future projects while building a better sister-brother relationship.

In October the artist duo collaborated again at The St. Louis Kids Expo. This gave them even more opportunities to paint live and meet other kidpreneurs. In December of 2018, Reagan and Logan attended the YBK luncheon where they received a certificate of recognition and were able to mix and mingle with kidpreneur friends to learn more about their businesses. They also worked on their slogans and "elevator speeches." Today, Reagan continues to book events and receive commissions from her teachers and Logan continues to work on perfecting his painting skills so he may too begin to complete commissions. It is a lot of work and time put into raising moguls and switching back and forth from mom to momager, but it can be done. So never think twice about giving your child the opportunity to explore entrepreneurship if this is something that they are interested in.

Taking that leap of faith and breaking the cycle!

Being a momager was one of the best gifts I could have given to my children, and I wouldn't change my decision to let my kids start their own business for the world. I hope that you will do the same for your child(ren). No matter if you're a single parent with 1 child or married with 5 children this will be hard, but it will also be fulfilling at the same time! It makes me very proud to see Reagan bloom into public speaking when asked about her brand. This was one of our challenges as even though she is a people-person, like me, she has a fear of public speaking. With more exposure and opportunities to share her talents, she is slowly getting into the groove of things, and plans to host her first paint party in the near future. Logan has some super cool ideas for 2019 as well, which includes comic books. I cannot wait to see their growth!

I encourage you to take that leap of faith and introduce your child into the world of entrepreneurship and financial freedom! If you have already started that journey, kudos to you and remember to surround yourself with like-minded individuals who will support and motivate you to keep going. Seeing your child grow into a little boss, learning to come out of their shell to socialize with customers is the coolest thing ever. Just know that you can achieve all the goals that you have set, trust the process, commit and create a circle of bosses around you and your family.

You got this mom! Good luck to you and God Bless!

"Just Keep Swimming" -Dory

For more information contact:
Latrice Floyd
Destined2paint@gmail.com

Shay Danrich
Author, Entrepreneur, Momager

Shay Danrich is an author, entrepreneur and a momager, who is dedicated to helping her son succeed in business. Her professional career spans 20+ years as a business management consultant. She enjoys working with entrepreneurs and small business owners and has made a remarkable name for herself throughout the Saint Louis Metropolitan Area. Shay's positive influence and optimistic views are priceless. She keeps her integrity and genuine passion for everything she's a part of.

Today, Shay is focusing her efforts on a new venture named "Mr. Fresh." Mr. Fresh is an Air Freshener and Deodorizer business started by her 10-year-old son Joshua Danrich, a young entrepreneur.

As his business momager, Shay is providing a professional business acumen and dynamic energy as

an entrepreneur to help train and develop Joshua,
while also teaching him how to build and operate a
successful small business.

Shay holds a Master's Degree in Management from
Fontbonne University.

I Am Shay Danrich –Mom Boss

Finding Success: Entrepreneurship
Through Adversity
by Shay Danrich, MMgt

*"A leader is one who knows the way, goes the way,
and shows the way." – John C Maxwell*

Hello everyone. My name is Shay Danrich. I am
a single mom of an incredibly gifted young
entrepreneur named Joshua (a.k.a. Mr. Fresh). He is
10 years of age and is the owner of Mr. Fresh. Mr.
Fresh is an air freshener and deodorizer company
that launched October 20, 2018, and it was on that
day, Joshua entered into the fantastic world of
entrepreneurship, and I became a momager, "Mama
Fresh."

Why did we launch an air freshener and
deodorizer company? Well, if you ask Joshua, he
would say, "Mr. Fresh was birthed from a lifelong
love of all things automotive." —and I truly agree.
So, when he asked me if he could open a car
dealership, I sought after a stepping stone or two, a
bridge perhaps that could get him there. A way of
aligning him with the fulfillment of his dream of
owning a business today. This caused me to spring
into action to make his dream a reality, and
Mr. Fresh was born.

So, what is it like being a momager of such a young entrepreneur? Well, I'm glad you asked. It's fun, rewarding and sometimes challenging. It's like a rollercoaster ride, full of highs and lows with plenty of learning experiences. I never thought in a million years that I would be a momager of a 10-year-old entrepreneur —and if, I had it to do all over again, I would.

I have recognized what Mr. Fresh has given Joshua as a person and an entrepreneur. As a momager, I see an entrepreneurial outlet for cultivating his creativity, business chops, and the opportunity to teach him how to engage and build rapport with others. As a mom, I see my son becoming more patient with himself and others, building self-confidence and great self-esteem. Win, Win.

Entrepreneurship in Motion

When I look back at my childhood, I can see the path that shaped my becoming an entrepreneur. I truly enjoyed nurturing and helping people excel at whatever was essential to them. My teachers, fellow students, and family members often referred to me as confident, courageous and a natural born leader. But, I was also said to be bossy and strong-willed.

Today, that energy has been transformed into being a good delegator and someone who is focused, creative, and highly strategic respectively. And I just realized something. Being called strong-willed was a lovely way of saying I was a bit stubborn. That's funny.

I developed all my brightness and interest in making money and became my own boss, by merely following something my family always told me when I was young, "Believe that you can do anything and you will." I believed I could help people and now I do. This belief helped me to form entrepreneurial traits and characteristics that have transformed me into a mom boss. As a momager, I've observed Joshua exemplifying these same entrepreneurial traits and characteristics which have transformed him into a boy boss.

As an entrepreneur, I've enjoyed educating and giving advice to others. I believe knowledge is power only after it has been put to use. Once a person becomes educated, the next step is implementation —putting all that new knowledge into good use. What about you, what knowledge do you have that can be put to good use today?

Fork in the Road

"Turn your wounds into wisdom." – Oprah Winfrey

In 2016, I lost my job and joined the ranks of the unemployed. This placed a huge hardship and financial strain on my household. I struggled with making ends meet and moving forward in life — and to make matters worse, Joshua began to struggle academically in school. I remember thinking, "What else can go wrong?" —And it did. Murphy's Law states what can go wrong, will go wrong.

In 2018, I learned that Joshua was going to have to repeat the fourth grade. Having to repeat the fourth grade was a devastating blow to both of us. The news caused Joshua to become withdrawn and dispirited. He lost hope and felt like a failure. He didn't think he could or felt like he should go on. He felt like his life was over. His heart was broken —and as his mom, I knew I had to do something, but I didn't know what to do. I just knew that I couldn't and shouldn't give up. I knew this situation had to take precedence —and everything else was secondary. What would you do, if you were faced with such a great challenge?

Moving forward, I began to guide and encourage Joshua. It was important that he knew we were in this together. I told him that he had to look at the situation from a different perspective. With a new set of eyes. I told him that failure was not the end and he was given a second chance — a fresh start. He could begin again.

Even though I could see the hurt, disappointment, doubt, and despair in Joshua's eyes, I continued to encourage him —because, if at first, we don't succeed, we must continue to try, and try again. No retreat, no surrender, because, nothing beats trying, but winning. So, we must always try and repeat until we succeed.

That day, I told Joshua a secret. One that very few know or understand, which is this, "Things rarely go as planned." This is because; often we have no plan, to begin with. We have just an expectation or desire to accomplish something great, and then, we chase after it. However, what happens when one has a plan that fails? Well, that's what Plan B is for. Plan B is the pivot to a new path to get across the bridge to the other side, whereas, the other side is the success.

Hope is never lost, it's just not always found in the choices and plans we make. Hope is not still where we wish to find it, but it is always there. Hope is our way, and the obstacles we encounter, only present us with opportunities for greater hope. What do you hope for? What do you wish you'll do someday?

Time to Teach

"Humility is absolutely necessary for true learning."
– Robert T Kiyosaki

As a parent, it is imperative to teach life skills that develop the whole child which requires critical thinking, problem solving, creativity, and understanding in order to equip them to become leaders in this ever-changing world.

Joshua's personal development, education and equipping him with the tools and techniques to be successful in life are significantly very crucial to me. But, as you can imagine, it's easier said than done. Being a single parent and a mom presents a unique set of challenges.

As a single mom, I am Joshua's only parental source of emotional, financial, spiritual and physical support, and stability. Acknowledging and understanding this huge responsibility meant that I had to be extremely resourceful and patient, in order to produce the results we needed day by day. Knowing that I might not always accomplish my goals, I sometimes had to take stock in what was learned in the process. I got really comfortable with that notion, because, with every adventure, comes the opportunity to learn something new and useful.

Sometimes, we learn more about the marketplace, systems and process; but other times, we learn something more about ourselves. However, not everything we learn can be used right away, or within the current cycle or span of time. Some things are merely made perfect for future events —like a fantastic solution or answer to "x" just sitting on the shelf waiting for the opportunity to complete the equation and make someone shine.

The next thing I am going to say is critical and should never be forgotten. "Every failure is gain." That's right. Let me say that one more time. "Every failure is gain." Would you want to know why? Every failure is gain because it is the identical twin of success. They're both merely feedback.

I am teaching Joshua to be his own person. The best possible version of himself that he can be — that he would let his light shine, be seen by all men, and reach his full potential. Potential is an exciting thing. Like learning, potential has no age limit; so reaching one's potential starts to materialize the moment that one begins the process, and is realized at the end of the race.

I am also teaching my son to be mindful; that is, self-disciplined and reliant, dedicated and genuinely focused in each moment to which he stands -whether he is standing alone or within a group. I want him to change the things, he can, leave what he can't change to others that can, and to be wise enough to know the difference between the two.

New Mindset

"Beginner's mind doesn't mean negating experience; it means keeping an open mind on how to apply our experience to each new circumstance." – Mary Jaksch

One of the hardest things to do in this world is to start over. It feels like such a daunting and impossible task. I've had to start over before, and now I am helping Joshua to do the same. I had to get him to change his mind so he could succeed when he didn't want to. He has such a unique ability, but he was also a little broken down. What he needed was a shift and not a reality check. He was already standing in the paint. I just needed him to believe in something he could do, do well and make his presence felt.

I remember when I had to face some of the biggest and challenging moments of my life, and I had to change. I was sitting in a sandwich shop trying to pull myself together, and that caught the attention of a man sitting a couple of tables over from me. To make a long story short, I met him and his wife for coffee, and that man became my coach. His name is Don Wilson, who goes by the moniker, "COACHDON." Don Wilson is a transformation coach, who specializes in personal development, achievement and growth. I mention him here because he helped me start over and achieve the current mindset and success I have today.

I have learned that success is not achieved only by what we think we can or want to do —or because we believe in ourselves or because we are smart or highly educated; but by how much we are willing to change, to attract the kind of success we desire. Did you know, that what we experience and feel can build confidence, and that confidence with the right mindset, can attract success? It's true.

So, I had to be mindful, very intentional and strategic about how to love and provide the appropriate guidance to my son that would engage him and change his mind. We were standing at a very critical point in our lives, and I knew it was vital that we stay focused, moment by moment — and always to move forward and leave yesterday behind only taking what is needed from yesterday into tomorrow.

I also learned to consider Joshua's worldview and present mindset, which, in simple terms is the way he views the world —and his mindset is his perspective on reality; how he thinks and feels about his experiences. This is how people young and old filter their worldview —through how they feel and think about each and every experience had. Albeit, personal, educational, professional or otherwise.

Armed with this knowledge and understanding, I was able to see, to some degree, how easy it was for Joshua just to give up after he learned he had to repeat the fourth grade. At that time, the goal then became, "How do I help him start living again? How do I redirect his energy in a positive, confident way?"

Birth of Mr. Fresh

"You have to aspire to something so great that you have to have God's help!"– Steve Harvey

Now the real work had to begin. To engage Joshua, and hopefully redirect his energy, we had to work together. First, we acknowledged the situation we were faced with. Next, we set attainable goals. Last be not least, we committed to executing the pathways to obtain our set goals. As Joshua's mom, I knew that school alone would not be a fix all remedy for him because he dreaded going back. So, combined with school, I sought other opportunities that would motivate Joshua –such as his lifelong love of cars. Win, Win.

Armed with this valuable information, I enrolled Joshua into a program called Young Biz Kidz (YBK) for entrepreneurial youth. This gave Joshua an outlet to explore and learn more about his passion of cars. Then I did business research and sat with him day by day to discuss my findings and recommendations. Little by little Joshua began to awaken —and met the idea of building a business around auto fragrances with zest and zeal.

Helping Joshua start his business meant I had to focus and have faith —and I had to be careful to maintain work-life balance. I had to parent when I should be parenting and be momager when I should be momager —and above all, remember he's only 10 years of age. So, it was imperative to remember that he is a child and not just any child. He is my child and a gifted young entrepreneur.

The mission I chose to accept was designed to rescue Joshua from the hurt and pain he was feeling. Through this mission, Mr. Fresh became a business and our mantra, "Faith to Rescue Every Son from Hurt."

As momager and financier, I had to tap into the knowledge and experience I possessed as a business consultant. Together, we had to plan, build, launch, manage and promote Mr. Fresh in the most efficient, cost-effective and profitable way possible.

I had to learn about a new business model and observe the competition. What's a business model?

A business model is normally, a single page design that depicts what a successful operation looks like. It identifies financials, both revenues, and costs. It describes the product or service being provided, to who and why. It even articulates market insights; where to market and who the customer and competitors are —and includes a team, vendors, partners, etc. —everyone that helps you to become successful in business.

I consulted my coach and filled him in on the adventure we'd only just begun. He is excellent with business models, and he provided some wonderful advice and set us on a path towards triumph. He took a look at our idea and costs and helped us design a unique business model of our own —which was complete with revenue and cost projections. He then recommended that within ninety days, we are to accomplish one of three things:

(i)   Break-even
(ii)   Break-even, and seek to discover the path to profitability, or
(iii)   get out and cut our losses.

Would you like to know what happened? Number two. No pun intended. We advanced beyond break-even, discovered our sweet spot and a path to profitability within the first 30 days.

Advice and Recommendations

"What you do has a far greater impact than what you say." – Stephen Covey

It took countless hours to develop the idea and to figure out what worked, and what did not, and it was well worth it. I believe in investing in my son, no matter the cost. There have been many challenges along the way. Thus, the importance of putting a system in place —and once that system was in place, everything started to flow much, much smoother.

No two businesses are the same. No matter how many companies you launch, each will have its own unique set of challenges, feedback and learning opportunities. Feedback and learning opportunities? Yes, feedback and learning opportunities.

Regarding feedback, there are two forms. "Feedback -- the kind you want to hear about and the kind you don't." Trust me, you want to hear it all; and the reason why is simple, "You never want to repeat what's not working, only what is."

In terms of learning opportunities, the great takeaway was what I learned from my young entrepreneur. He taught me how to support him.

110

This was important because I was on a mission to help him and not hurt or overwhelm him. Children experience stress, as do adults, and I chose to grow with my son and young entrepreneur —and I suggest you consider doing the same.

Do proper planning and preparing. Be it lean or full-blown. Let the business type define how far and wide you should go with planning and preparing. Know your numbers, your market (who your customers and competition are). Know your customers, because they help you answer the question of why, and your competition, because they are currently serving your customers.

Get professional help and support, whenever possible. My coach is a God-send. He has been a solid mentor, coach, and a dear friend. I have found that even those that have good judgment in business and have done well for themselves can only offer general advice. But, if you need a specialized touch, it's best to seek professional help. The return on that investment is worth it. You'll be glad you did.

Finally, be persistent. There is nothing you can do to advance your practice or young entrepreneurs' business better than being persistent. Not education, talent, smarts or success holds the power to get the job done. Only persistence. So, don't give up. If it's not working, ask why. If it's broken, find out where it hurts. Pivot, pivot, pivot. Don't get stuck in the mud. Remember, "If at first, we don't succeed, we must continue to try, and then try again."

Four Surefire Strategies That Put You In a Winning Position

1. Have a strategy, commit to it when it's time to scale or call it quits. But, quit, only after you have done your due diligence and have exhausted every avenue, path, and unturned stone.

2. Always remember, you can only attract success. You cannot buy it or find it. If seeking to see success is your approach, it will elude you.

3. Success, just like failure is feedback and will find you. No matter how hard you try to hide from the latter. Always listen to your market, so you'll discover the way to go. I did it, and you can do it too.

4. Succeeding as an entrepreneur is a personal achievement first, and then a professional one. It only becomes professional after you make use of it in business.

Journey of a Lifetime

Embarking on this journey has taken great courage and commitment —and the connections, mentors, coaches, partners, friends, family members, and experiences have all been instrumental in allowing this new path of life to happen. Thank you all for your love and support.

To all future mom bosses everywhere, I personally wish you well and suggest that you enjoy the ride. Good, bad or indifferent, it's feedback. Listen to it and heed its recommendations or warnings. I wish you all the best —and congratulations. Welcome to the club. I believe in you.

Follow the life and business journey of Mama Fresh and Mr. Fresh (Dynamic Duo) - We still have so much more to share, experience, do and see.

Learn more about her current venture, Mr. Fresh at:
www.BeFreshNow.com
or
Shay Danrich
Email: reachmrfresh@gmail.com

Nia Lewis
Entrepreneur, Momager

Nia Lewis is a wife, mother, entrepreneur, overcomer and now an author. Nia has worked hard to change the trajectory of her life. She evolved from being a statistic (teen mom) to a momager. Even though the odds were stacked against her, she is determined not to allow her past circumstances to stop her from achieving her goals. After moving from job to job she knew she had to make some changes. She was determined to walk into her purpose.

In 2010 she moved to Guam with her husband and children while her husband was in the United States Air Force. She met another military wife who was making cosmetics out of her house. Nia was so impressed by her neighbor's endeavors, the woman invited her to learn how to make lip gloss, nail polish and lipstick as well. Each day Nia would visit with her colleague and they would create new colors together. Soon Nia started to make products on her own adding her own ingredients and colors. Eventually she would introduce her daughters Nyla and Alyna to the art, teaching them to make many beauty products including lip gloss and nail polish.

When Nia is not making cosmetics, she enjoys teaching her children about generational wealth, saving and giving back. Nia also enjoys shopping and spending time with family

For more information contact:
Nia Lewis
nialewis898@yahoo.com

I Am Nia Lewis –Mom Boss

From Teen Mom to Mom Boss
by Nia Lewis

I never thought the day would come that I would be open and honest about my past. I have always been a private person, but now I feel it's time to share my story with others. Let's go back 16 years when I became a mother - specifically a teen mom. I had my daughter at 17 years old which led me to drop-out of high school in the 11th grade. I got my first apartment at 17 but was kicked out of my apartment 6 months later. I was devastated and fell into a deep depression while pregnant that lasted until I had my daughter July 24th, 2002.

The day I had my first daughter, I knew things would be different. I instantly wanted better in our lives. I decided to back to school to get my GED. Two weeks after giving birth, I started looking for GED classes and found one that would accommodate both mine and my babysitting grandmother's schedules. Over the next three months, I took night classes. It was finally time for me to take the GED test. I kept telling myself, girl you are not ready. I talked to my grandmother and mother about taking the test, they both told me I would be fine.

The day of the test I was so nervous I couldn't eat anything. Finally, I was called to the test administering area, took the test, and who knew, I passed with flying colors. It felt like a weight had been lifted off my shoulders. I couldn't wait to get home to tell my grandmother and mom that I had passed, to which they replied, "We told you that you would pass."

Sometimes you just have to take a leap of faith and do the hard thing no matter the outcome. If you don't, you will never know what you can accomplish. Just do it -- never give up. My story is for you if you feel stuck thinking there's no way out, and you feel like giving up on your dreams because you got pregnant at an early age or had any barriers to your goals. If this is you, then keep reading.

Facing barriers

Three years, after passing my GED, I went back to school where I met my husband Bobby (who was in the Air Force) and received my Associate's degree in the dental field. I would always tell him, "I want to be my own boss. I never want to work for someone else making them rich."

On April 20, 2008, we had our 2nd daughter Alyna. We were both happy, and Nyla was excited to be a big sister. I was still thinking about starting a business- a boutique. I was confident in my concept, but I was concerned about the location. I kept putting off my ideas while working in the dental field. I was unhappy going to work every day, working for someone else knowing I had all these business ideas.

One day my husband came home and told me he had received orders to go to Guam, overseas. The assignment would last for four years, and the girls and I could come with him. I had to talk with my grandmother first, who said, "Girl if you don't go with your husband, I'm going with him." My mother confirmed what my grandmother had told me. So, on October 10, 2010, we moved to Guam.

While there, I met a friend who made lip gloss, she sold it online through the Air Force business page, causing her to make at least $200 a week. I was immediately inspired to start an accessories business selling ladies handbags and jewelry. For the next year, Nyla and I did pop-up shops to sell to the local ladies on the island. On weekends my new friend would teach us how to make lip gloss so I could add it to our online business.

Soon after starting, my new friend got married to a soldier and moved off the island taking my inspiration with her. I didn't want to make lip gloss anymore so, I stepped away from it and started working on the Air Force base at the dental clinic. I worked there for 3 years, almost until it was time for us to leave the island. On November 4, 2014, we were still living in Guam when we got the news, it was time for Bobby to retire from the Air Force. He was excited to be getting out after serving 15 years and three months.

We did some traveling before ending up back in St. Louis. After six months of living there, I decided enough is enough -- let me write down my business ideas, my goals, and what I want to achieve. Remember, I said never give up on your dreams. So, I decided to sit down with Nyla and Alyna at the kitchen table one day to ask them how they would feel about making lip gloss again. They said, "Sure, sounds like fun." Alyna had always had a thing for lip chap, as she used to call it when she was three.

Planning for a New Endeavour

I suggested to the girls that we write a business plan. I had taken a class on the topic while living in Texas, before arriving back in St. Louis. We discussed researching the market, sales strategies, financial data, and more. We would need a mission statement and a pitch in case an investor wanted to invest in our products. By this time, they were looking at me like I was crazy. Writing a business plan was foreign to them at their age so of course they didn't know where to start and I didn't either. The challenge was on, we began writing a business plan, researching our products (including cost & quantity), learning to invest in the stock market and saving money to start a business.

When the time came to purchase the ingredients to make the lip gloss, I realized the vendor I had chosen also had supplies to make nail polish as well (hint: new product). When the supplies arrived, we began making our product samples on the weekend and testing them out. We would have glitter and gel all over the floor and on my kitchen table. Making lip gloss and nail polish is really messy! I made my daughters a Facebook page, and on the second day, they had 100 followers. I also made them an Instagram page. I was so happy that family and friends were actually supporting them as young entrepreneurs.

After being in business for about a year, and not making sales the way we would have like to, I met a woman, named Arriel. Arriel is the CEO of a nonprofit organization called Young Biz Kidz. She hosts classes once a month, teaching kids how to level-up on their business while learning financial literacy. Since joining Young Biz Kidz, my girls have learned so much about taking their cosmetic business to another level. She truly is a Godsend.

I want my girls to have what I did not have -- knowledge about self-love, saving for a rainy day, building generational wealth, investing in stocks and bonds, and the experience to open and manage a bank account. I want them to have a vision so big, that it changes the world one day. I hope that my story inspires others to never give up on their dreams. I journeyed from seventeen and pregnant to learning and continuing to teach my daughters how to build wealth, with help from our village (family and friends).

A lot of people counted me out but, I refused to be another statistic. I wanted to show my girls that through hardships, you can always bounce back and soar. I encourage them and you to write down goals, move to action and watch plans manifest. Speak positivity into your life. Don't hang around negative people. My grandmother always said, "Girl, you have to keep going no matter what. You can't wait for someone to do something for you. Do it yourself," may she rest in peace. So, I know I must show my girls that there will be tough times. Things will not always be perfect or turn out how we planned, but you will never know unless you jump, and take a leap of faith. If you don't take anything from this book, take – NEVER GIVE UP! Yes, you will struggle with doubt, I still struggle today but, I refuse to let the devil win. I pray about it and keep going. I have to -- I have daughters watching me.

Encourage Yourself

I thought, working a 9 to 5 was the only way to wealth until I realized that working a job makes the company you work for rich, while you're left to struggle and be the unhappy one. I want you to know that you are not alone. I'm sure you have a story to share with the world that might help someone who needs healing! This book is about *mompreneurs*, who have sacrificed their dreams to make sure their kids are living out theirs.

We want to encourage moms and dads to make sure they listen to their kids when they come up with creative ideas. Sit them down and guide them into writing down their plan. You would be surprised how interested they are to learn how to take their business ideas from a thought, to actually making money. My daughters, in the beginning, questioned how they would make money online and sell to people they don't know. Since then, they've learned the answer to those questions. Yes, you're going to get a lot of questions, but at the end of the day, they will have fun doing what they love.

"I can do all things through him who strengthens me." - Philippians 4:13

Landra Cannon
Learner, Momager

Landra Cannon is from St. Louis, MO and is a mother of two. Her daughter is a college student and her son is a part of Young Biz Kidz. She recently obtained her GED and is currently going to classes for credit and financial improvement. She has been a member of Higher Ground Community Outreach Center for two years going on three years.

In Landra's spare time she enjoys relaxing at home, reading, and spending time with her children. She is a devoted hard worker, who loves entrepreneurship and always makes efforts to motivate someone else.

Landra's goal is to one day learn enough about financial literacy that she can help others.

I am Landra Cannon –Mom Boss

The Cycle Stops Here
by Landra Cannon

"Train up a child in the way he should go [teaching him to seek God's wisdom and will for his abilities and talents], Even when he is old he will not depart from it." - Proverbs 22:6 AMP

As a mother, I wanted more for my children. I didn't want to make the same mistakes my mother did. I found myself remembering those exact mistakes and challenging myself to be a better mother to my children. Growing up being the youngest of four children my mother didn't take the time to teach us about finances, credit, money management, or even the importance of saving money. When I got older and became a mother, I found myself making the same mistakes with my child that my mother made with me. I didn't start to really get an understanding of the importance of teaching financial literacy until I had my second child and found myself a church home. However, I still couldn't show my children anything because I didn't have enough knowledge in me to pass on to them. Immediately I realized that this was something that I needed to take to prayer because I wasn't comfortable with staying in what almost felt like an impoverished state. My family has had so many generational curses (an evil that's passed down from one generation to another) it was time to end the cycle of perpetual poverty. With Jesus' help and prayer, doors began to open that would ultimately start to break the curse of poverty that had covered my family all these years.

Laying the Foundation

One Day I was sitting on the couch looking at Facebook on my phone and saw Arriel Bivens – Biggs, CEO of Young Biz Kidz, an organization that teaches kids winning strategies in money and business. After seeing this, I decided to talk to my son Darrel about business ideas he might have. Darrel told me he wanted to own his own construction site one day and he wanted to help people less fortunate to rebuild the communities. I thought that was a very liberal idea and I was extremely proud of him. I didn't know much about owning a construction site, but I did know he would have to know about money to pay his employees, buy equipment, save money to start his business, and so much more.

After joining Young Biz Kidz my son was so excited, anticipating our first meeting as a new member. He was now able to join other kids that had great businesses or was in the process of creating a company like my son. I thought to myself "WOW, I cannot believe we are actually doing this." To see my son participating in the class really warmed my heart and the fact that Young Biz Kidz program helps kids learn how to manage their money was even better. "Great!! This is just what he needed!" I said to myself.

Facing Fears

Starting out, Darrel was shy in the meetings, especially when it was time to speak in front of the class or take pictures. As his mother, I began to question if I had made the right decision for him. See, this was out of his comfort zone, and I didn't want him to feel discouraged or forced, but I also knew in the back of my mind I wanted a better life for him than I had. I have learned the more wretched life is, the more I can grow and see Jesus was always there to help me. In His word he states, "I will never leave you nor forsake you" and I am a living witness through experiences that this is true.

Darrel was in front of the class and YBK members were taking turns introducing themselves and stating what business they'd chosen. Darrel was looking around nervously awaiting his turn when Jesus sent him help through the supporting voice of Mrs. Arriel. She immediately saw an opportunity to help Darrel and began coaching him through his shyness. Mrs. Arriel told him it was ok and that because he was new, it was understandable that it would take time to get comfortable with everything. Darrel started to speak loud and clear. I was amazed at how precise his speaking voice indeed was. After going to some classes, it was time for Darrel to present his business in public. However, there was one small problem, my son wasn't a construction owner yet. We needed to sit down, come up with something he could sell now and begin learning everything he needed to help him on his journey towards ownership in his construction business later in life.

A Super Idea

My son and I came up with many ideas for his first business (selling food, selling candy, we even thought of selling socks) but finally settled on a lemonade stand. Simple and easy was the first thought that came to mind. The next step was finding a location, which easy because Young Biz Kidz provided that. Then, Darrel had to come up with a name for his lemonade stand. Since he is a big fan of the Avengers, he came up with the name Super Lemonade. He said it was because the heroes in the action movies have powers and he thought that was super cool. I personally did not like the name at all, but Darrell and my daughter love the Avengers so much, I knew for a fact that my opinion for the first time just didn't matter. His heart was set on SUPER LEMONADE!

Soon after, I began to send out flyers through text messages to family and friends and posted on social media. Everyone needed to know about Darrel's unique lemonade stand. Darrel said to me, "Mama this is kind of like advertisement." I replied, "Advertising is what we are doing." Darrel also needed items to make the lemonade: lemons, sugar, sprite, and of course water. His sister's favorite drink is lemonade mixed with sprite, so she asked him if he could have that as another drink to sell! Darrel absolutely loved the idea and came up with the name Doctor Strange for this delicious but bizarre combination.

To be very honest I didn't have any money at this time, so I had to come up with a plan to get the items he needed to sell his lemonade. Immediately my mind said, "It's time to hustle." One thing I taught my children, is how to hustle and that is precisely what Darrel and I did. People tend to associate hustling with something negative which just isn't always right. Hustling is merely a form of obtaining the things you need through action or persuasion.

Darrel started by calling his father for help who gave him 30 single dollar bills. Cool, that's done! Next, I called our family for items such as ice, lemons, cups, etc. We didn't have to spend one dime for him on products to sell his lemonade because everything was given to him. Darrel learned how to hustle by asking for help and telling others about his business. The night before it was time to sell, Darrel began taste testing his lemonade. He added, then took away, added less, then added more...we were tasting lemonade all night. We sampled so much lemonade, if I'm being honest, I became sick of lemonade, but it was worth it seeing him smile and having fun while making it.

Finally, we came to an agreement that the lemonade tasted great! THANK YOU JESUS! The special day was here, we were so excited and ready for lemonade in one capacity or another! TIME TO SELL! We packed up everything early so we wouldn't forget anything and headed out. I asked Darrel how he felt about going to sell lemonade for the first time. He said he was glad and was ready to make money to save. I told him he would have to invest some of the money back into his business and Darrel was very cool with that.

Making the Sale

When we arrived at the marketplace, Darrel setup all his items for the lemonade stand, then stood back, looked over his table and noticed it was a little bare. He asked his big sister if she would go to the store to get him a few more items for his table, and she agreed. Darrel asked her to bring back action figures only to go along with the Super Lemonade theme, and it worked out perfectly. She brought back all the Avengers flags, two Avengers cups to sit on the table, and so much more. He was thrilled! Darrel was ready to sell and make some money!

As I sat there observing, I noticed Darrel being a little shy again. I understood this was his first time and his shyness was to be expected, but I wanted him to have a great experience. As customers shuffled through, he answered questions about his business. He would sometimes stumble on his words because he was nervous. He even looked back at me like *mama help*, and I would say "Darrel tell them more about your business." I wanted him to be able to talk on his own and eventually he did. The less I helped him, the more he did what was needed. Darrel kept selling, and after a while, he almost became a natural at handling his money and making drinks. He was running his own business, and I was excited for him!

At one point during the day, Darrell even learned a little about making deals with the other kids who were selling as well. One of the Young Biz Kidz didn't have enough money for a cup of lemonade, so he decided to strike a deal with my son, "if you give me a cup of lemonade, I will give you a candy bar," and my son told him, it's a deal. That was too funny to me to see two kids doing bartering transactions like grown-ups.

It was so hot that day, lemonade was right on time. Darrel had already made thirty bucks maybe more. The cups we used were 12 oz. Styrofoam to keep the ice from melting. Darrel decided to sell the lemonade for one dollar a cup. In addition, to my amusement, Darrel came up with the idea to sell ice for a dollar. I was both shocked and amazed when people actually bought ice for a dollar. I looked on with pride at my Biz Kid who was selling, bartering and even taking pictures during the event. I honestly felt like a PROUD mother.

Afterward, Darrel was excited to count the money he had made. It came to a grand total of (*drumroll please*) $67. Since Darrell had only spent ten bucks he had borrowed from his sister for decorations for his table, he was able to give it right back to her and have a profit $57. After all the preparations, the setup and the sales, Darrell planned to manage and distribute his newly earned income. He paid tithes first, then took some of the money and invested it back into his business, paid himself a portion and put some into a saving account that accumulates interest, so he was still making money. That boy even asked me if I needed any money! (*Kids, you got to love them.*) Allowing my son to be a part of Young Biz Kidz has changed our lives. As a mother, I can say that I made the right decision letting Darrel join the class. He is learning how not to have to struggle making financial decisions and how to get answers to his questions about his own money. Darrel came to me and said, "I have confidence mama, I don't fully understand, but I am getting an understanding."

Building on Success

Even though Darrel is still a part of the Young Biz Kidz, he spends time drawing and building as well. He draws all kinds of shoes, shoe designs, buildings with City Skylines and he has a fascination for Minecraft. Darrel does side jobs as well, like cleaning, helping family members, and doing small errands for his big sister to earn extra money to add to his savings. I am just so grateful for the Lord, allowing and giving me the opportunity and the courage to share Darrel's story.

My prayer is that this story will be able to help another mother out there, who felt the need to make a difference in their children or child's life. The best thing we have learned and will continue to learn is the importance of wisdom. When we were putting this whole thing together, figuring out what his business was going to be, then actually making the lemonade stand, we always had to use wisdom. The goal is and will forever be, not just for him to make money and be financially stable, but for him to also one day pass on his knowledge to his other little cousins and friends so they too can help break generational curses of poverty and become leaders.

I have come to the realization that age just doesn't matter once God has called you to be a leader, you almost don't have a choice but to step into that leadership position. To become a leader is precisely what I wanted for my son. If I would have allowed my previous circumstances to hinder me from becoming a better mother than what I had growing up, then Darrel would have never gotten the opportunity to experience what it feels like to be a young entrepreneur. This journey thus far, has been a complete learning experience for both of us. It has allowed us to learn so much about each other, and we both are growing in knowledge, and I am looking forward to what God has in store.

For more information contact:
Landracannon1@gmail.com

Cecelia M. Rigsby
Administrator, Child Advocate, Momager

Cecelia Marie Rigsby is a devoted woman of God,
wife to Michael Rigsby, mother of three
Michael Jr, Mikaela Rae and Michelle Rigsby,
daughter, sister, and friend. She is an
administrative assistant with the St. Louis Public
School District.

Cecelia worked in the field of education for over 25
years, assisting students in grade levels from
preschool to high school. She studied Early
Childcare and Development education at Central
Methodist University where she earned a
Bachelor's Degree. Prior to that, Cecelia completed
her Associate Degree from St. Louis Community
College at Forest Park.

While working in education, Cecelia received a number of honors including the Pacesetter Award, Employee of the Year, and Teacher of the Year.

Due to her passion for working with children and families, Cecelia is the CEO of her family's consultant, training, coaching and mentoring business entitled, *Sources, Empowering, Emergent, Develop (SEED, LLC)*.

Cecelia also loves working in ministry, praying, singing, encouraging others, motivating people, feeding the homeless and caring for those less fortunate.

When Cecelia isn't working, she enjoys selling jewelry, spending time with family and friends, attending church, and serving others.

Cecelia believes that it is better to give than to receive, which is why she actively looks for ways to bless others.

Cecelia's mission in life is to be the best servant that she can be for the building of the Kingdom of God.

I am Cecelia Rigsby –Mom Boss

I'm a Mom Boss!
by Cecelia Rigsby

*"For I know the plans I have for you," says the
Lord. "They are plans for good and not for
disaster, to give you a future and a hope."
-Jeremiah 29:11*

Being a mother can be rewarding, fun, a blessing,
entertaining, liberating, joyful, and hilarious. BUT in
keeping it very REAL being a mother can be
downright HARD. I often ask, "Am I doing this
mother thing right?" I know the Bible says God has
plans to prosper me and not to harm me, plans to
give me hope and a future (Jeremiah 29:11), but
training up a child in the way she should go
(Proverbs 22:6) is an ongoing process of coaching,
mentoring, listening, caring, sharing, monitoring,
and balancing. Parenting can be overwhelming; that's
why I depend on God every step of the way as I
navigate being a parent and a "Mom Boss!" Allow
me to share a little bit of our entrepreneurial journey.

Getting Started

My daughter, Michelle "Shelly" Rigsby came
into entrepreneurship through my mother, Katherine
McHaynes. Shelly is a social butterfly who loves
meeting new friends, interacting with others, sharing

ideas, and is always up for a new challenge. Knowing this, my mom is always looking for exciting opportunities for Shelly. One day she was introduced to Young Biz Kidz (YBK) Entrepreneurship Program. After meeting with the YBK team she spoke with me about Shelly starting her own business and registered her to take part.

Shelly, my Mom and I decided because I had my own business "CeCe The Jewelry Lady" it would be a great idea to spin off Michelle as "Shelly the Jewelry Girl." Along with building, promoting and launching my jewelry business, I would have Shelly work in her workshop creating bracelets about three times a week. Shelly's bracelets ranged from $1-$4. Her materials and supplies were bought at a low cost while family and friends gave her items they were not using to build her stock.

We quickly developed Facebook pages, websites, and more to market our businesses. Every vendor event I could find for us to attend I jumped at the opportunity for us to make money. Some we visited together while others we did separately. If I could not participate in a vendor event with Shelly, I would have my mom or my husband, Michelle's dad, take her to make money. Soon Shelly was in every entrepreneur program I could find for her to learn and grow her business. We were off and flying high doing great things and making lots of extra cash.

From our sales, we would first tithe back to God and split the rest, 50% in our pocket and 50% back in our businesses. *(We try to save but are not always successful.)* Shelly quickly developed a sense of pride and admitted she believed the best part of the business was making money…"cha-ching!"

So everything was great…right?

As a new business owner and an entrepreneur's mom, I realized at one point I wasn't enjoying myself as a boss mom of a young entrepreneur. I was frustrated and not liking the overloaded process of continually going from selling events to selling events. I had to re-evaluate what we were doing as mother and daughter to live a balanced life with our church activities, ministries, school work, rest time and more. We were into too much, and if I didn't find us some balance --quickly, we were headed for disaster and burn out.

Learning to Balance

Some years ago, I recalled the Lord dealing with me about "chasing money." I saw how I was leading my daughter into doing the very thing God told me not to do. "Chasing Money!" I had to narrow our plans because, I worked full time and at the time, Shelly was a 5th-grade student.

I work twelve months a year in a school district and now focus on my jewelry business sporadically. Shelly only promotes her business during holiday seasons and during the summer when she is out of school. The newly limited time allotted to our businesses now helps bring balance to our lives and keep us from "chasing money" and also keeps us on a path of enjoying life. As a Mom Boss it is my responsibility to keep us organized and that means I have to put plans and systems in place to keep us from going into overdrive. I'm very good with schedules, routines, and order.

I narrowed Michelle down to one entrepreneur program (YBK). The YBK program fits into our plans perfectly. Shelly is able to enjoy getting together with the young entrepreneurs once a month and attend quarterly market places where she is able to sell her jewelry products. This routine helps me as her Mom Boss to not be so stretched that we are not adequately resting or missing out on things we also enjoy doing such as going to the movies, celebrating at Six Flags, shopping and attending church services.

Staying Focused

Shelly must know how to read and write to do business, and I do not want her focus to move to money while rejecting her school education. I want her to know the importance of making money and working for herself but not at the sake of no longer qualifying for honor roll, school clubs, perfect attendance, her enjoyment of school and just being a kid. As a Mom Boss, I supervise her study time which on average requires her to do 2 to 3 hours of homework per night. Everyone needs balance, and as a woman and mother, I want us both to know the importance of living a balanced life. Yes, it is nice to earn extra cash to save, tithe, shop, go out to eat, enjoy movies but everything has to have balance.

Lesson Learned

In conclusion, I had to go before God and ask for direction with our pursuit of entrepreneurship. God reminded me that He has plans for our lives and what God has for us is for us. The Lord told me to cease struggling and allow him to lead me every step of the way in all areas of our lives including our businesses goals and dreams.

Cecelia can be reached at
cecerigsby@yahoo.com
rigsbycecelia@gmail.com
or you can review her jewelry website at
cecetjl.weebly.com

CONTACT INFORMATION

Mission- Young Biz Kidz (YBK) nonprofit's mission is to presents a positive, diverse and creative way to teach youth business and financial education. YBK's purpose is to create a challenging interactive environment that prepares youth to effectively maneuver finances, encourage leadership, heighten critical thinking while, guiding them into entrepreneurship.

Young Biz Kidz

website: youngbizkidz.org
email: youngbizkidz@outlook.com

AUTHORS

Aunkule Benford-Campbell

aunkule@att.net

Arriel Biggs

arrielbiggs@gmail.com

Landra Cannon

landracannon1@gmail.com

Shay Danrich, MMgt

reachmrfresh@gmail.com

Sauywanna Davis

swaunnie01@gmail.com

Latrice Floyd

destined2paint@gmail.com

Cecilia Grigsby

cecerigsby@yahoo.com

Tamishio Hawkins

tdhawkins83@gmail.com

Nia Lewis

nialewis898@yahoo.com

Tanika Prowell

jz.sweets@yahoo.com

Tamara M. Robinson, MBA

tamararobinson.consulting@gmail.com

Made in the USA
Columbia, SC
06 May 2019